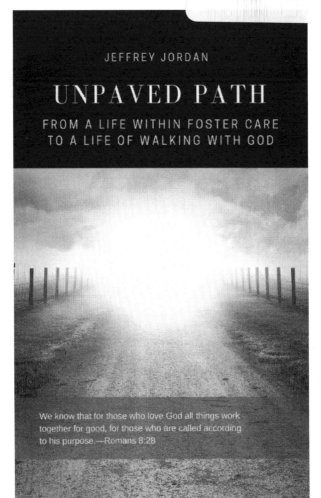

JEFFREY JORDAN

UNPAVED PATH

FROM A LIFE WITHIN FOSTER CARE
TO A LIFE OF WALKING WITH GOD

We know that for those who love God all things work
together for good, for those who are called according
to his purpose.—Romans 8:28

i

UNPAVED PATH

From a Life Within Foster Care to a Life Walking with God

Jeffrey Jordan

Christian Publishing House
Cambridge, Ohio

UNPAVED PATH: From a Life Within Foster Care to a Life Walking with God by Jeffrey Jordan

ISBN-13: 978-1-945757-28-0

ISBN-10: 1-945757-28-0

Table of Contents

Acknowledgments

I don't even know how to begin to thank the many people who played a role in both my life and the completion of this book.

-There is my wonderful Savior Jesus Christ. You helped me through every second of my life when I wanted to throw in the towel. You have always been great to me. Your grace and power will always hold a major part in my life. Thank you, Jesus, for allowing me to put my thoughts on paper to write this book.

-To Michael Edwards, thank you for guiding me through the dark times in life and you never stop believing in me.

-To Melissa Robinson, you believed in me since day one. You help lead the direction of promise side of my life. Thank you.

-To Kristin and Keith Bridgman, thank you so much for your care and support through different times in my life. You guys gave me a chance when we first meet at Starbucks.

-To Jeremy Taylor, you believed in me first hand to take me right under your wing, to teach, and guide me through many things. I am glad to call you my friend, mentor, and brother in Christ. Thank you.

-To Sue Jensen, Sue Bryant, and Village Manor, you all saw something in me and gave me a chance. Your faith with helping me along the way with the book is so grateful. Thanks.

-To Betty Bastin, the love you share every time we speak just a blessing to have. You are the real "mother figure" in my life, and I am so thankful for our relationship.

-To Tony Evans, thank you for them strong, true devotions every morning to get my day started.

-To Mary Cotham, I just thank you for believing in me and taken a risk with me as I complete this book.

-To Andrew Hart, thank you for keeping me grounded and checking in often on the book. Great friend you are. Glad to call you my friend and brother in Christ. Thanks.

-To my church family, Living Hope Baptist Church thank you for being with me through life and helping see God's vision to better myself every day.

-To the editors, I just thank you all for taking the time out of your days to read and help me get this book published.

Introduction

Because I came into this world in a hopeless set of circumstances, living through one heartache after another, it was my greatest longing to give others hope where it may have seemed like they had none. After a few years of feeling this hunger, I came to realize that God could use me to help others, as well as help myself along the way. Many times, it is as simple as listening and showing that I care for them. There is no greater joy than giving of oneself to help others who are struggling with family issues, or a financial crisis, even depression. However, an even bigger joy is helping someone find his or her Savior, Christ Jesus, or help someone within the church who may be struggling with life. Throughout this book of an unpaved path, you will see my journey from a path that began in difficulty, distress, and suffering, which has since been conquered, leading to success and achievement, as I seek to give back to the local community, helping the next generation.

April 14, 1992, was a warm, breezy day. It was one of those days that should have been spent in a park with a few friends, sharing a picnic together. However, one young mother was doing no such thing, as she was about to give birth to her second child. This child was coming into the world alone, not to be lovingly held, or cared for, not as a bundle of joy but rather with no loving relative to witness his birth. There are many reasons for this, of course, which we will get to soon enough. My mother was this young woman.

Suddenly, there was screaming and crying that could be heard throughout the hallway. My young mother, as she lay there, about to give birth was in tremendous pain. At 1:15 PM, I came into this world weighing 8 pounds 1 ounce, with big brown Franklin Hawkins eyes. Yes, that was the name that I was given. Now that the painful delivery was over, my mother (Donna) wanted nothing more than some peaceful rest with just her and me alone. However, as you will learn, alone time was not going to come.

My mother was originally from Columbus, Ohio. She lived alone. In fact, she was a bit of a loner, having few friends if any. She had done most things by herself, preferring it that way. In many ways, she was different than most. My mother would eventually come to live in Hamilton County, also known as "Sin City," Cincinnati (before Las Vegas). She struggled to keep a job, so she found herself on welfare and living in community housing. These conditions she brought on herself by the decisions she made. Nevertheless, she walked around mad at the world, as though it were everyone else's fault, frustrated because there seemed no way out. Life was not kind to my mother, which she fueled even further by using drugs as a coping mechanism. The necessities of life, such as food, clothes, and sadly, drugs were here main priorities. For these reasons, she lived a life of poverty, never seeking help to climb out of the hard times.

My mother avoided her family at all costs because of her drug addiction and felt that she would be judged harshly for her lifestyle. She spent most of her time in and out of Jail beginning at the young age of seventeen. This was inevitable because of her drug addiction, no employment; the only recourse was to steal to support her habit. Sadly, she became satisfied with a life of drugs and crime, finding shelter, food, and friendship with fellow inmates while being incarcerated. Her last visit before the judge, he warned her that continued trouble was going to get her a 3-5 year prison sentence.

And so it would be, it came true, my mother was sentenced to 4 years in the Ohio Department of Rehabilitations and Corrections. She just was not able to break her addiction to drugs. The judge had hoped that she would change her life around, so he sent her to a treatment center. However, throughout her sentence, she did not improve, and her health just worsened. She refused to own her problems, never seeing her actions a negative, criminal behavior, refusing to accept help.

In October of 1991, my mother's stay in this rehabilitation center changed course, as she informed the staff that she was three months pregnant. The correctional facility had to test her because she had been there far longer than three months. They feared who the father might be, after establishing that she was only three months along.

My mother met with her counselor week after week, never giving them any information as to who the father was. She believed that she could game the system by getting pregnant, as they might cut her sentence short. Well, she was correct in a sense, once the investigation showed my father to be a correction officer, they did not release her but transferred her to another treatment center. Even more, she needed to accept help to get her life turned around because she now had a baby on the way. Our Creator sees every life as precious, so there was hope for this life growing within my mother, all he would have to do is accept that path.

My mother was transferred to the Franklin Pre-lease Jail Center, which wasn't far from the rehabilitation center. When asked about my father, she'd say, "I don't want him in any trouble or to lose his job." This really reinforced my belief that my father had been a correction officer at the rehabilitation center. I felt that it would be impossible to know who it was because there were likely many black officers working the center at the time. Because my mother would be giving birth to me while still serving her time in jail, she wasn't going to be able to keep me. Even at this low point, my mother refused to reach out to family or friends, letting them know what she was going through, giving them a chance to be there for her. Legally, and sadly, she had the right to keep the identity of the correction officer from the authorities. Also, she was not obligated to let me go stay with family and friends. What was really going on with my mother?

What is a truly loving family?

If a child is not given the love, guidance, principles, morals, and values that they need to function, he or she will be unable to have any kind of meaningful friendships, relationships, or normalcy throughout their childhood right up and into adulthood. This is why persons like my mother fall through the cracks of society because they do not have, for they were not given the coping skills to function within society. Clearly, my mother never received those things, so how could she have ever passed them on to me?

Jackie Stewart, Living Hope Baptist Church, Recreation Center Director

Many babies that enter into foster care come away with one tragic story after another. On Texas judge wrote of foster care, the state has created a situation where "children have been shuttled throughout a system where rape, abuse, psychotropic medication, and instability are the norm."[1] Unexpected events[2] allowed me to escape any such heartbreaking events. My foster parents had been married for sixty-four years. I was raised with love and support and was given guidance, principles, morals, and values that allowed me to have meaningful friendships, relationships. While I did not resent the fact that I was expected to attend church, it wasn't until I got older that my appreciation and live for Jesus Christ grew, where I fully committed by life to Him.

My faith in Christ is the pillar upon which I have laid a foundation for life. It was because I

---

[1] Judge Rules Texas Foster Care System Unconstitutional ..., http://www.impactfund.org/social-justice-blog/texas-broken-foster-care-system (accessed November 05, 2016).

[2] Ecclesiastes 9:11

came to recognize that Christ took my sins upon himself and died on my behalf that enabled me to have the life that I have today. Jesus has made it possible for me to have a righteous standing before the Father. My heart is filled with gratitude to Christ. He has become my example, the life for which I try to pattern myself after. I have shared the same love and caring that my foster parents gave me, as well as the same expectations, having Jesus Christ as our guiding light.

My girlfriend, Jewel, personally loves God and is a woman of great faith and devotion, which is what makes her a truly beautiful woman. Having her serving God alongside me has made my path even easier, which I know is pleasing in the eyes of God. Both my girlfriend and me have an inner satisfaction of knowing that we are helping others and, most of all are doing what is pleasing in the eyes of God. Jewel knows that she is very dear to me and, even though we are not married at this point, I follow the Apostle Paul's counsel, "husbands should love their wives as their own bodies. He who loves his wife loves himself. For no one ever hated his own flesh, but nourishes and cherishes it, just as Christ does the church, the two shall become one flesh." (Ephesians 5:28-29, 31, ESV)

If I can be considered successful, it is entirely due to the Lord. I have taken advantage of every unexpected event in my life where His servants have offered me a hand up. I was placed on the path to life early on and for this, I am very grateful. I have tried to follow His teaching, have worked diligently, and have pressed on toward the goal. I follow the Apostle Paul's example, "I do not consider that I have made it my own. But one thing I do: **forgetting what lies behind** and straining forward to what lies ahead, I **press on toward the goal** for the prize of the upward call of God in Christ Jesus." (Philippians 3:13-14)

Paul was speaking of his goal of sharing with Jesus in the Kingdom of God. He used the image of a runner, who is running a race, hoping to win the prize. The runner never looks back at who is behind him. Paul to does not look back, allowing his mind to be clouded with past memories. Paul, like an athlete, strains every muscle in his body to attain the goal. He has his eyes focused on the finish line. Paul removes the thoughts of his persecuting the church. He sets aside the painful memories of being imprisoned and physically punished for the faith. Like him, I do not allow the painful life of my biological mother, how I came into this world, to keep me from looking ahead. Whether I am completing school, competing for a job, seeking a promotion, or an election, I have trusted Jesus Christ for the outcome and have accepted His will, I have kept my eye focused in front of me, the goal that lay ahead. The Bible gives a very clear path to follow for life, and although it may be difficult at times, I trust God will guide me. Many people in my life have played a role in helping me to find that path. If I can offer any suggestion in this book, it is this, many opportunities come at us in life, and many people are a part of those opportunities. We need to recognize the good from the bad and take advantage. Below are just a few people that have had a tremendous impact on my life, I took advantage of those opportunities that they offered me.

Jason Pettus is the pastor of Living Hope Baptist Church

Spiritually speaking, this man has taught me how to grow more spiritually and personally. He has become like family, who has connected me with the larger church family. His support cannot be overstated, and will always be appreciated and pass forward.

Bowling Green, KY City Mayor, Bruce Wilkerson

The mayor helped me to find the appropriate centers within our community that deal with juveniles. The city gave me the Jefferson Award, which is for outstanding community service. For these and other things, I am deeply grateful to the mayor.

George Fant of the Seattle Seahawks, the starting left tackle.

He is a good friend of mine through our church activities. He has offered me great advice and counsel through the year, as we talk quite often.

Kyle Barron is the Direct of Student and Engagement at South Central Kentucky Community and Technical College in Bowling Green.

He is a friend and mentor, who have offered me sound advice on life. He has financially supported my work and aspirations. For these things and more, I am deeply indebted to him and his wife, Kristine.

CHAPTER 1 Jail Time

One of the first names recorded in the Bible is that of Seth, meaning, "He set or appointed" or "replacement." Eve, Seth's mother, explained why she chose that name, saying, "God has appointed me another offspring in place of Abel, for Cain killed him." (Gen. 4:25) Noah was the son of Lamech, tenth in line from Adam through Seth, whose name means "rest." Lamech said he named his son Noah because "This one will give us[3] rest from our work and from the toil of our hands arising from the ground which the Lord has cursed." (Genesis 5:29, NASB)

The Father himself changed the names of some of the Bible's most significant men and women for prophetic purposes. For example, he changed the name of Abram, meaning "father is exalted," to Abraham, meaning "father of a multitude." His name, Abraham became prophetically true, as he was the father of many nations. (Gen. 17:5-6) Think too of Abraham's wife, Sarai, when God renamed her "Sarah," meaning "princess," referring to her becoming an ancestress of kings. (Genesis 17:15-16)

---

[3] Lit *comfort us in*

When a newborn baby is delivered anywhere here on earth, often the parents give much thought in choosing their name, searching through books and now the internet. However, my mother already knew what she wanted to name me. She wanted to write it on the birth certificate before sharing it with the doctors and record office. As she was writing my name, the doctors seemed worried at just how long my name was going to be. She ended up giving me a name that everyone in the room wishes they had control over, which was Franklin Hawkins. One might think in a way that this was prophetic too, as there was a bit of irony in my being given that name. Franklin is the transferred use of an English surname originating from the Middle English "frankelin" which was borrowed from the French "franc" meaning "**free**." However, she named me "Franklin" after the center where she was now living. I have often wondered, "Why would she do that?" Clearly, my mother needed much help in those days. It would seem that she just did not care. This was her last time to hold me and it would be her last time.

As many hundreds of thousands of other foster children, I would not initially know what a stable family was. Because God is outside of time and he can look at the stream of time, he can see me years down the road, knowing if things will get worse, remain the same, it improves. Me, though, I could only see the here and now, wanting desperately to know who my biological parents were and why they have left me in the foster care system. I had many people coming into my life during that time, and I was not able to understand why, what their agenda was and why they wanted to be in my life. As I got older, the moving from home-to-home began to get stressful. All I wanted was a stable, faithful, loving family. From chapter 2 forward my use of the word "mother" and my use of the word "father" will refer to my adoptive father and mother, as I view them as such.

CHAPTER 2 Cincinnati Ready

Most of us in life come to a point when we are young and realize what we want to do with our lives, and this was no different for me. Of course, having no family to love and care for me as a child played a significant role in this new revelation. However, maybe I am getting a bit ahead of myself here, as I just was not to the point of being able to determine what I wanted as of yet. The things that I daydreamed about were what a perfect family might look like. I also thought a lot about running away. The idea of a perfect family was vital to me. As I came across others in my life back then, I just wondered, "wonder who truly does love and care for you?" The other youths in my foster family helped me to realize that I was not alone in this.

The big change in my life came in 1994. I was still in foster care at that point, living in this home with many other kids just like me, with some who were bigger and some who were smaller. Those who were bigger were allowed to stay out later, as I remember it. This foster home accepted children anywhere from six months to 18 years old.

There was one person who would come to the foster home almost every day to talk and play with the kids. This individual was there so often, one might have thought that he lived there or something. Over time, I noticed that he chose to play with me outside more and more. Over a two-week period, he started having more and more conversations with me. While he spoke English, I was just not getting what he was saying. In my mind, it could have been that he was saying to go hide while I count to ten. Anyway, I was standing there, pulling at his pant leg, wanting to play more. The next thing I knew in my young life, I was getting water balloons thrown at me, I was enjoying ice cream as it ran down my face, playing in fenced in neighborhoods.

In other words, my life had taken on a new change. I was not certain where I was, but I believed I was still in Cincinnati. Now, I had six other people that I lived with, as this family adopted me. Jeffrey and Tonya were now officially my legal parents. They had four biological daughters of their own, which meant that I now had four sisters. This meant many more days of playing with water balloons and eating ice cream.

My new sisters were Teaira, Ciara, Latoya, and Lationa. With being adopted my name went from, Franklin to Jeffrey. Which was kinda cool but weird. Now, I had to start going by a new name that I didn't even know how to spell, but it was okay with me. I was named after my adoptive father. During his visits with me at the foster home, he was looking for a boy. While he truly loved his daughters, he wanted a boy. All, I knew, at the time, was, I was now a part of a new family and still lived in my hometown.

From the very beginning, I became "daddy's boy." From the day I started pulling on his pant leg, I was seeking to follow and be led. With my being their only son, there were a few different expectations.

CHAPTER 3 Welcome to the Family

The one thing about family that brought me the greatest joy was knowing that my father was there every step of my life. Even at ten-years-old, I could appreciate this. When my behavior started to change towards him, mother, sisters, church family, and school, my father was still there to guide me. He would always want to know why I did what I did. This one time I had to cut the yard, a yard that was a beautiful mini football field. The yard was cut in wavy lines, and it was wonderful to see when the sun hit the grass, which was very nice to me. My father was the lead music director at our church, and I could not wait for him to get home. I could not wait to see his proud facial expression as I showed him the front and back yard. I was slow to show my mother anything because she could find fault in anything. I decided to play some basketball out front while I waited for my father to arrive. The fun days of being ten and not having to worry about the complicated things adults faced every day, just having a fun day in the sun.

I saw some neighborhood friends playing outside, and I told them "whatever you do, do not run in our yard please." I was sweating my but off putting the yard stuff up in the garage when I heard kids nearby running. I could hear some boy tell a girl "don't run that way!" The kid said it loud like it was an ice cream truck coming.

The girl refused to list to him or my stern warning and ran right through the yard. I looked at her long hair and thought, "we will see how she likes being bald." I picked up a lighter I saw and did not give it a second thought of hurting this young girl. I started chasing her wanting to burn her hair. I finally caught her and had a piece of her hair, I noticed that everyone was watching, frozen in time as it were. My father had gotten home in time to watch this entire escapade unfold in front of his eyes. Her parents were hysterically running over, and my Father just told me, "go in the house and wait for me in the kitchen." As I headed for the house, I could hardly hear things being said behind me because my heart was beating so loud in my chest, I was sure it was going to burst out of my chest any moment. Once inside the kitchen, I watched wonderingly as the young girl's mother was wagging her finger in front of my father's face.

It just got worse, as I saw police cars pulling up in front of the house, talking to the girl and her parents. The fear level just escalated, as I knew this was not going to be good. I saw the officer now talking to my father when I was summoned to come back outside. How did this go from a great day of high expectations, wanting to please my father, to now standing there as I received that intense look of my father that would put the fear of God into you? I am standing in the middle of this hectic scene watching the young girl, her parents, the police officers, and my father trying his best to reason with the unreasonable, hoping to keep the cops from taking me downtown to the juvenile detention center. Sadly, seeing the facial expressions and the intense back and forth, my fear was that I was heading downtown.

Again, things went from bad to worse, as the one person who never advocated for me came into this chaotic scene, my mother came home. She had that look as to why police cars were sitting in front of her house. She pulled my father to the side to get him to explain. As I watched, my father go through today's events with my mother, she was not looking at him, her glare was laser focused on me. I could see the furious, anger in her face. To say that my mother could not stand me being her child would be an understatement. She walked toward us, looking me up and down, saying nothing to me, and here it came, she turned to the police and said, "take him away, he needs to be other troublemakers like himself.

Being just ten, I was at a loss as to why mother would treat me the way she did sometimes. My father, my greatest advocate, kept trying to change their mind. However, it wat to no avail, as the police placed me into handcuffs, place me in the back of the police car. Stunned, my semi-blank mind was thinking how lose these cuffs were around my wrists. The being taken downtown did not turn my life around, likely it just made things worse, as my behavior did not change. I will say, I was embarrassed to be in the back of that police car, as people passed in their cars, they stared through the windows, looking at me, as though they knew exactly what I had done. I even had a schoolmate next to me, shaking his head. I didn't know what to expect when got out of the police car.

CHAPTER 4 Learning the Lesson

As we pulled into the Juvenile Detention Center, the first thing I noticed was the wired lines running around the building. Then, there was the pin pad that one needed to unlock the door. One would not think the weight of a massive, heavy steel door opening and closing could be determined by its slam, not to mention the intimidation of such a sound. It can and it does! Once inside, the only thing I could think of is, 'Oh, how I wanted to be outside, back mowing the yard, or out front of my house playing ball.'

There is a smell that goes with a detention center that is found nowhere else in the free world. Maybe it is the smell of body sweat and fear, but it comes back throughout life, as occasionally you will be doing something and that scent hits you, bringing back those unpleasant memories. As they were booking me in it was nothing but chaos, with footprints all over the wall, teens screaming and cursing at each other. The physical check for contraband or a weapon was nothing I wanted to repeat ever. They make you run your fingers behind your ears, through your hair, and yes, just like in the movies, you must expose your privates, and if you do not know what the phrase "bend over, squat, and cough" means, Google it. Just make sure you are not doing an image search. The good and the bad of it was, I had time to appreciate my freedom (the good) because I went in on Friday, which means I would not see the judge until Monday (the bad).

The two days I spent there was nothing short of a mini horror story for a ten-year-old. Let me just say state clothes will make you miss freedom, with their bright orange shorts, a white T-shirt, and white socks. Of course, nothing fit; all of it was too big. I was placed in the single-man cell, which brings me back to the scent of the place once more, it is now intensified a thousand fold, with a mixture of urine and other body fluids that we will leave out here in this book but was certainly present. Trust me; I did not turn the light off. One thing most people do not realize, a ten-year-old, who has some troubles adjusting to life, is far different from the seventeen-year-old that is in that same detention center, who is truly a gangbanger and thug, talk about scared straight!

That first evening at the Detention Center, I had to speak in front of a group and explain why I was there. Talking aloud to others about pressing matters, even just one person is something that I had never been comfortable with unless I was acting out a class clown. By the time I had to head for my cell that night, I knew I was very wrong for what I had done. I also knew that to continue down this same path; it would lead to nothing but self-inflicted pain, heartache, and loneliness. I worried about what the judge's role would be and just how much trouble I was in for the entire weekend. I had gotten the break I had hoped for the whole weekend, Monday; the Judge released me to my parents. Both of them came to pick me up at the Detention Center, where I anxiously awaited to be released. My mother still had that look, as though she wanted me to stay right where I was, and she was forced to come get me.

Before delving into the next paragraph, let me offer some insights into the impact that a lack of love can generate, not to mention, no love couple with a pure hatred being imposed on you every day. While I am certainly no childhood mental health expert, I can offer what little I know. When a baby is born, it needs certain things from its environment, so as to grow up and be a functioning young adult. If this stuff is withheld, he or she will become dysfunctional. This is why you find some teens that are antisocial because they do not possess those life skills. Think of the teen movies that give us the different cliques in high school. Some of the more common types of cliques found include: jocks, tomboys, cheerleaders, mean girls, foreigners, gamers, hipsters, hippies, troublemakers, peacemakers, class clowns, "cool kids," arty intellectuals, gangsters, "ghetto kids," stoners/slackers, girly girls, punks, preps, goths, skinheads, geeks/nerds, and drifters. Are any of these teenage cliques "normal"? No, many of them are joining certain groups because they lack the life skills and are trying to find some measure of comfort with others who are like-minded.

The Bible actually deals with this, as it deals with an infinite number of challenges that we face in our human imperfection. My new friend, Edward Andrews, has often stressed to us in his many books that we, all people, need to be aware of the level of our human imperfection. He writes, "We are all mentally bent toward evil (Gen. 6:5; 8:21), with a treacherous heart that is desperately sick. (Jer. 17:9)"[4] The only thing that will counter a child who has been brought up in an abusive or loveless environment is the love and life skills that remove bent thinking and replace it with rational thinking. Proverbs 23:7 (KJV) says, "For as he thinketh in his heart, so is he." In other words, how you think is how you feel. In the Bible, we are given the life skills that enable us to "put off the old man [person] with its

---

[4] Edward D. Andrews: *THE BATTLE FOR THE CHRISTIAN MIND: Be Transformed by the Renewal of Your Mind.* Cambridge: Christian Publishing House, 2016. P. 09

practices and have put on the new man [person] who is being renewed through accurate knowledge" of God's Word.' (Col. 3:9-10) The apostle Paul says elsewhere, "take off, according to your former way of life, the old man [person], who is being destroyed according to deceitful desires, and to be renewed in the spirit of your minds, and put on the new man [person], the one created according to the likeness of God in righteousness and loyalty of the truth." (Eph. 4:22-24) Keep these biblical principles in mind as we continue with my unpaved path.

After my brief moment in the Juvenile Detention Center, my mother's love, if there was any before, was never to be seen again. I watched my father, who looked sick, with a face that seemed swollen, from stress and anxiety. My father only ever wanted me to turn my life around, which I felt that I was honestly trying to do. Every encounter with my mother was nothing more than a beat down emotionally, mentally and physically. She would literally sit on my face so that I could not breathe and hit me over the back. She did not talk to me, she screamed at me. She would humiliate me by making me eat standing up while everyone else ate sitting down. She made sure that she drilled into my mind that I would never amount to anything in my life, reinforcing at every turn that my life would be spent behind bars, where I belonged. She says she lost love for me, but I had wondered just where the love was, to begin with, as I had never felt it. I was only ten-years-old, coming from abandonment and she never gave me a chance, nor helped me to recover from those experiences, but rather placed me in yet another evil life experience.

The lack of love and the lack of life skills brought out the worst in me as I was just looking at everything in life as a joke. If I saw an old woman fall out of a wheelchair, I would not rush to help her. No, I would laugh at her. If my mother knew that this was the child that I had become, she would have ramped up her torturous tactics for sure. Returning to the clique mentality of high school that I mentioned above, I spent my time with other kids that just did not care about life, which made me feel the same. The one drawback to being a troubled child is, if I acted out, my father cut me off and did not give me the attention that I would have liked to have had. I knew that if I acted out and were caught, there was a beating waiting for me. However, unlike the children that go unpunished today, I know that I deserved a spanking. Know that, I am not advocating beating children but rather appropriate corporal punishment does mold the mind as you warm the behind.

My mother was an example of excessive punishment as she sat on my face, cutting off my air and beating me as hard as she could, believing that this was best for me. However, those beatings were not sufficient because they were not going to stop me. Being ten, I could not understand this violence toward me. I came to this family when I was just two years old. Even still, I felt lucky to come to the family that wanted a boy after having four girls. I was lucky that they were close friends with my former foster parents, taking me in 1994.

I learned of my biological family when I was in third grade. My parents tried to break it to me gradually, giving me information here and there and showing me a picture of some lady weekly, a lady that I never really knew. However, this attempting at helping me understand where I came from was not helping me get off the path that I was on, a collision course. My behavior was out of control in every aspect of my life: in school, at home, and in the church. By the time I was in the fifth grade, you could not tell me anything, as I was a Mr. know it all.

CHAPTER 5 Mr. Know It All

I started my day knowing I was going to wreak havoc on other people's lives. When I got on the school bus, the first thing I would do was bully the younger kids. I refused to sit in my assigned seat, and I would talk back to Ms. Rose (the bus driver). These were the ways that I chose to start my day and I had not even arrived at school yet, where I knew that I was heading straight to the principal's office. At this point in my young life, I had not mastered the art of empathy, so I really did not care about the pain that I was causing others. Or was it that I did not fully realize the damage I was doing to others and myself? Mind you, I was only in elementary school at this time.

At times, I wondered if my older sisters were in on it with my mother, as they showed no indication of being concerned about the abuse that I was facing. In my mother's mind, twisted thinking as it was, she believed that if she brought the fear of God into me by her beatings and punishments, it would scare me into staying out of trouble. Little did she know, this was one of the biggest contributing factors to my getting into trouble, it was just a vicious circle. Maybe it was my twisted thinking too because I felt she did not want me to grow and improve and that is why she was so cruel. My father, my defender, and advocate would talk to her about me, trying to get her to see the light that there were other ways to correct my behavior. Sadly, mother was not having any of that. It was coming time for me to leave elementary school and my teachers were certainly glad to see me go. I did make an effort to tell my favorite teacher, Ms. Green, showing her the bruises and whelps I was getting at home. Unfortunately, even she did not believe me, so whom was I going to go to, no one, right!

Another piece of emotional, embarrassing baggage was my problem of wetting myself when I took naps or went to sleep at night. My father seemed too busy to help me. My mother would give me a hand all right, as she made me stand in front of the bathroom toilet from sunset to sunrise. As I stood there throughout the night, my uncaring family slept the night away peacefully without concern for me. I can remember the times when my father made an effort to check on me. I would hear him coming up the wooden steps, but he would never make it because his legs would start to swell and go weak. I felt terrible, believing that I was contributing to his poor health. My mother and sisters would wake up and see my father that my father was trying to check on me, as I stood there naked in front of the toilet, emotions flooded through me.

Imagine the stress of being beaten, wetting oneself and being beaten some more and the having to stand naked in one spot all night, and now having to go to school. Any rational person can see why a child might act out, seeking attention from others. My causing havoc in class, refusing to obey my teachers was not getting through to them that things were not good at home. As I pointed out earlier, if a child from birth is not given the tools of love, empathy, guidance and direction, counsel, he cannot reciprocate these things to others. If a puppy is kicked, not loved, and abused his entire life and he then bites someone as an adult dog, should anyone be surprised? Thank God, we do not put down children and teenagers like those that do dogs that bite others. I even stopped listening to my father as he was getting sicker and he too was making me angry. I was only ten years old.

My home life was truly a torture chamber now that I look back on it. I never slept in my own bed, a very nice bed I might add. I was only allowed to sit on it, nothing more. My mother made it so that I could not lay on it to watch TV or play video games like other kids. Every night I either slept on the kitchen floor or stood in front of the toilet naked, leaving me sleep deprived through my childhood. This was punishment because I still wetted to be or on myself even if taking a nap. I now know that "Abused children may display behaviors shown at earlier ages, such as thumb-sucking, bed-wetting, fear of the dark or strangers. For some children, even loss of acquired language or memory problems may be an issue."[5]

As I lay there asleep or even pretending to be asleep, my sisters would step right over me, not a care in the world. I felt like nobody wanted me there. I felt like my only purpose was to labor around the house; clean the cars, clean the house, and clean some more. As the days passed, nothing ever got better. I was ready to leave at age ten. In some ways, when I graduated from elementary school, it played a huge part, as I felt like I was going away to college. On graduation day, both of my parents were genuinely happy to see me move on. After pictures had been taken and I said my goodbye to my teachers and classmates, my parents pulled my aside to tell me some good news. They were going to allow me to invite friends over and go to Six Flags Kentucky Kingdom. It almost seemed unreal. I was so

---

[5] Signs of Child Abuse | Child Abuse Prevention and .., https://www.brightfutures4kids.org/learn/signs-of-child-abuse/ (accessed November 25, 2016).

excited to get home, get out of my dress clothes and play with my friends.

This day was even better because my father's health had improved. My mother even allowed me to sit in the passenger's seat as my father drove. When we pulled into the driveway, I rushed to my friends' houses to see if they would be allowed to go with me. The two friends who could come were surprised. It seems that the parents in the neighborhood were ready to forgive my past bad behaviors. Honestly, in my heart of hearts, I do not want to be known for hurting people and causing trouble or even to make my parents look bad. That day went well, me, my friends and family had a great time. However, the fear of getting into trouble was in the back of my mind all day. I knew trouble found me; I did not have to go looking for it. Well, I did not have to wait long, as trouble found me the next day when I failed to take out the trash and watch the dishes. Mother came down into the basement with that look in her eye. I knew there was something that mother wanted out of me; I just never knew what it was.

CHAPTER 6 Behavior Issues

Summer was upon us, and I could not wait until the school year started; I was going to be in the sixth grade! This meant a new school and new friends. Sadly, even though my mother made no progress in her dealing with me better, I made no progress in improving my behavior. It was summer, and I had nothing to do, like summer camp, so it was time to act out some more. Even today, I cannot explain why I would think like that. My thoughts that ran through my head were so negative.

I knew in the back of my mind that I was going to be gone from the house of pain because I was going to run away. Let me start by saying, unlike Huckleberry Finn and Tom Sawyer, I was not very good at running away or getting into mischief. I was caught far more than I got away with things. I ran away six times and was caught every time. The cops were called the third time. There they were, the police that is, and all I had to do was tell them of the abuse. But how?[6] I just could not bring myself to do it at this point.

---

[6] When I was a child, I wanted to tell of the abuse at home but did not know who to trust and how to tell. I felt that I would not be believed and when my favorite teacher did not believe me when I broke down and told her, well that just reinforced this mistaken notion. My advice to any child or woman in an abusive relationship, tell and

The police stood there giving me their stern warning, "Do not leave the house without your parents' permission"! As they said those words, I was mentally plotting my next escape. I looked over at my father, I could see how sick he was, and I have felt that I am the reason for his getting sicker by the minute. So, my running away is twofold: I did not want to remain in this house of torture, and I did not want to continue to contribute to my Father's getting ill. Yes, now, I know that my father was suffering from kidney disease, fighting for his life for fifteen years. The thing is, when you are a child, you just do not know the reality of the what and why of it.

I did make an effort and straightened up for about two weeks. Being good, it made those two weeks drag like an eternity, though. Sometimes I would sneak out of the house to go nowhere. I would just stand or sit outside of the house and watch. Other times, I would run to the park, staying there until I felt like going home. At times, my mother and my sisters would come looking for me, and I would stay hidden, watching them from the shadows as they searched. They would be at it for an hour, and I did not care. I knew what awaited me at home and this would force me to stay even

keep telling until someone believes: friend's parents, teachers, guidance counselors, the police, children services, a pastor, and so on.

longer. In my childlike mind, this abuse was all right; it was what every kid received from his or her parents.

There were times when I got home from school and none was there, my mother had not gotten home yet. It was but a brief moment in the chaotic times, but it felt good at that moment to have no one screaming at you, telling you how bad of a person you were. I would throw my backpack on the kitchen table and run around the house screaming and rejoicing, living in the moment. I was so worn out from the mistreatment, and moment of relief was a bit of paradise. The more of these moments that I experienced, it moved me to want to act better and not have my family be mad at me for my small mistakes. If I could just show my family that my acting out was not going to last forever.

If it has not been made clear up until this point, as many may be asking, which came first, the chicken or the egg? In other words, did I start acting out and then my mother started punishing me or did my mother start punishing me and then I started acting out? From the moment that I entered my adoptive parents home, Jeffrey and Tonya, from the age of 2-11, I was mistreated by my mother. She detested my presence. She just wanted it to be her and her four daughters. She physically, mentally, and emotionally abused me almost from day one. I acted out because I was not loved, I was hated and detested. Abuse begets abuse, and so this is why I picked on the younger kids on the bus. I know some readers may feel that all of us are responsible for our actions, and this is true but remember that I had mistreated from birth forward and was given absolutely no life skills, no love, and so I could not reciprocate what I did not have in my toolbox. In all likelihood, my mother was abused somewhere along the line, and this is why she abused me. It does not clear her because she was an adult abusing a child and adults have the means of growing and improving their life skills. Of course, until someone tells them otherwise, it may be that they think their way of punishing or acting is normal.

Returning to the account, my friend's parents were friends with my parents. I was not allowed to stay the night with my friends, as my parents did not want me out of their control. I now returned to getting into trouble. It pained me as I saw how much my mother loved church and her daughters but detested my existence. My parents would mistreat me in extreme ways for small errors that all kids make, and parents should be able to help them grow out of these adolescent childish behaviors. My growing as a person just was not going to happen in this house. It seems like things grew worse still after they told me about my biological mother. Most kids never think this would happen to them. One moment your mom and dad are your parents and the next they are not but they are. My beatings grew so fierce that I was bleeding from them. It seemed that she was just not going to stop.

Some of the things I enjoyed as a child was improving myself, growing personally, not making the same mistakes repeatedly. Another thing that I enjoyed was my visits to my grandparents (adoptive) house for two months in Cincinnati, Ohio. I grew up in a big family, and the two-month visit every summer to their home brought me such relief.

While I was with the grandparents, it seemed there was always something to do every day, with all of the cousins, aunts, uncles, and friends. I remember one particular Saturday afternoon when I came back to their home after being at the pool half the day, and saw that they were having a yard sale. It was a big deal; they had everything you could want or expect to see at a yard sale. My grandparents were always excited to see me for the summer because I was always willing to help them with anything they needed.

Anyway, this Saturday, I was helping with the yard sale. My grandmother sent me down into the basement to get the chicken hen vases that she collected. I just could not believe that she was putting these in the sale. After getting these outside, I looked around at all of the stuff in the sale. My eye caught sight of a set of handcuffs, thinking this will entertain me for a while. When no one was watching, I shoved them in my pocket so I could play with them after I finished helping with the yard sale.

As the sale got underway, I hoped they would not see the handcuffs were missing. I did have what some might call "sticky fingers" as a child. I was prone to take things that did not belong to me. I mean I knew it was wrong, but I was moved to do it anyway. Anyway, I went into the house, I took the cuffs out and cuffed myself to see how the bad guys must have felt when they were caught. Well, stupid me, I hardly ever thought beyond the moment of immediate enjoyment because I could now not get out of the cuffs and the idea of a key dawned on me like a ton of bricks. How could I have done this to myself?

I did not want to go to my grandparents, but I had no choice. I have no memory before this where they had ever gotten upset with me, but somehow I figured this was going to do it. I went walking out into the middle of the yard sale, and I walked right up to my grandmother with the cuffs exposed. She looked down at me and said, "Kahlen (pronounced kay·len), take them off and put them back where you got them." I said, Granny "I can't." My nickname was Kahlen. My parents wanted to call me Kahlen on my adoptive papers as my official name but decided to go with my father's name, Jeffrey. Anyway, my grandmother was not happy, as she tried to conceal it, but I knew she was disappointed. Once my grandfather saw the predicament, he was in a hurry to find the key.

There was no luck in the search for that key. As the search went on, my wrists were getting numb from a lack of circulation. I told grandmother, and she began to worry even more. Because of me, the yard sale now turned into a scavenger hunt. As they looked for the key, I sat there on the porch, ready to cry at any moment. I now had a small taste of being cuffed like a criminal, having no way out. Once they determined the key was not going to be found, they decided to take me to the emergency room. They threw a sheet over the cuffs, to conceal my stupidity. I felt like the emergency room people were going to think my grandparents put the cuffs on me for some reason and blame them. I felt like they were all thinking, "What is this kid problem?"

Fortunately, the ER security was there, and they pulled out their key and took the cuffs off me.

Well, I now knew that any handcuff key would unlock any pair of handcuffs. I started rubbing my wrists hoping that they would be fine. My grandparents unlike my mother did not bring up the handcuff incident as a means of making me feel stupid. They were just worried and wanted me to be okay. If this incident had happened at home, my mother would have left the cuffs on until she had to take them off as a way of punishing me. My grandparents were the best.

One of the things I learned that day was, think before you do something. I learned to consider the whole of an action before jumping right in for the immediate joy of the moment. Of course, I would still rush into things. Still, the lesson was a planted seed. We all grow day by day, it is a lifelong process and children are slow to put these lessons into action. So, yes, my behavior deteriorated before it would get better. It got to the point where the doctors wanted to give me medications and visit with me monthly. I truly needed to change because that sounded like a terrible idea.

CHAPTER 7 Was It All My Fault?

Once I got back into Louisville from visiting Ohio. I knew something was up, my parents were sending me to another camp for the remainder of the summer. In my mind, my behavior and attitude had improved. It seemed as though my grandparents had thought it was better not to share the little adventure with the handcuffs. I was ready for my parents and me to start over, to improve and become a better family. I was not sure why they were sending me away again when I had only been home for one week, though.

As we drove up, I could see that my parents taking me to this brown and green building. I could see many kids my age playing kickball or tag, as we looked for a parking place. They had not mentioned how long I was going to be staying, but the two full bags of clothes should have been a clue. It seemed like my parents had sent me to summer camp. There were many kids there my age, and we did many fun things like played football, basketball, fishing, movies, and so on.

Many camp workers drove us to these places, paying our way everywhere we went. Each night before bed, they would walk around counting us, making certain that we were all accounted for. Some of the workers were talking with each of the kids one-on-one each day. The next thing I knew, a tall white guy with blonde hair was standing before me, introducing himself as the case worker for this building. He asked me into his office, where he asked me, "Do you know why you are here?" I replied, "This summer camp is a lot of fun." He explained to me that was not in some camp but rather my parents had put me on report. He scheduled me to an office visit with him two times every week, to talking about my attitude, behavior, and learning how to handle my problems. It was actually working; I could see changes in myself. After three weeks, he said that I had improved and that I would be seeing my parents tomorrow.

The next morning, I woke up very excited to see my parents. For an eleven-year-old boy, a month without seeing family seemed like an eternity. The place I had been staying in was actually beautiful. I mean even the breakfast was pretty much whatever I wanted. Everyone there seemed so proud of me, and they had helped me to make many adjustments in my thinking, feelings and behaviors. As I got dressed, my mood was getting better by the minute. I knew my caseworker was on his way to pick me up, but I also knew he was usually late, and this time would be no different.

I was actually trying to make time go faster this morning, but a watched pot never boils. As I waited for the moment I was back with my parents, I was very impatient once it seemed to take forever. It seemed like time moved according to everyone else's desires. I went and ate breakfast; then, I got all of my things packed and cleaned my room. As I stood looking at the place that I had been in for a month, I was surprised that my caseworker had not shown up yet. I mean he was usually late, but this was his best record. When he finally did arrive, I was so excited about him being there I forgot he was late. Loading the van with my stuff was a tremendous undertaking. It seemed like I was carrying things up and down from the Empire State building.

As I loaded things, I started to worry a little, 'why was he taking me home?' 'Why were my parents not picking me up personally, if I was just going home?' I thought I would finish loading things before asking. After loading everything, I spent some time hugging workers and saying good-bye, which caused me not to focus on why they were giving the ride but to just endure the wait even longer. It was nice hugging everyone, who had helped with my life changes, which actually lead to my better understanding the direction I wanted my life to go.

Once the hugging was out of the way, my impatience was returning, it was not even morning any longer. I felt some comfort when my caseworker started to drive; at least he was heading in the direction of my parents' home. I again just thought I would wait until I got home and skipped over asking about his driving me. Eventually, we were heading downtown; it was busy, so traffic slowed. Does it not seem like traffic is against you the moment you are in a hurry to get somewhere. I kept telling my new self, just be patient.

As I was watching out the window, I could see that the Jefferson County Hall of Justice courthouse was coming closer by the minute. This was not looking good. "Why would we be going there," I wondered. I had never been in the building, but I did know that it had courtrooms. My caseworker looked over and said, "Your parents are in the building, so we must go in to meet up with them."

Well, at least that sounded somewhat more hopeful. I was excited to see my parents and it seemed like that was just not going to happen. I stepped out of the van, and there was someone new, who was apparently taking over my case according to the conversation. I was introduced to the new caseworker. We were in the parking garage for about five minutes, In other words, another moment of what seemed like an eternity. The two caseworkers were laughing and talking, even trying to engage me in their conversation, likely hoping it would relax me more. All that was on my mind was seeing my parents. I know many might be thinking, with all of the torment from my parents, with the peaceful two months with my grandparents, with the months at this placement center, why on earth was I in such a hurry to return to the torture chamber?

First, it is all I knew. Second, I thought my new self would be the substance that would make our family better. Third, I thought my parents were ready for a change in the way things were. However, it would be some time before I understood it was them not me. Anyway, it seems that my parents were just late and that was what was holding things up. And to think of how great this morning started as I was enjoying my breakfast. I was starting to lose hope. As I waited achingly, the elevator doors opened, and my parents stepped off, my confidence returned once more. I saw them, they saw me, so I ran to them with open arms.

They seemed as though they were genuinely excited to see me. They even told me how much the family had missed me. We were laughing and talking, sitting in the courthouse waiting, and I now knew that my parents were taking me home. Then, the new caseworker came over, looking to talk with me some more, wanting to get to know me better. I was all talked out at that point, and I just wanted to go home. As the caseworker asked me the questions, I saw my parents talking with some man in a nice, navy blue suit. They did not come over toward me at all. Hope was fading yet again.

Eventually, my parents heading into the courtroom, as did I but not together as I thought would happen. I ended up between the two caseworkers. I really had no clue as to what was going on, and no one was in a hurry to tell me either. In due course, my parents were in the courtroom without me, while I sat outside in the corridor with the caseworker that had driven me to court. It was like wait, hold on some more, and finally, wait, even more, topped off with know nothing.

The two caseworkers were talking with me for a while and then the new one wanted to know if I wanted to go get a snack. I did not want any such thing; all I wanted was for my parents to come out of the courtroom. Sadly, they did come out, they did not come over and hug me goodbye or talk with me, they did not even look at me. As I stared at them, my new caseworker tried to explain what was going on but I did not hear a thing, except that my parents were never coming back.

I knew that my new and improved behavior was going to give way to the old me because I was an emotional boy. It all just seemed so unreal. I did not think my actions at home were so bad that they would no longer want me as their child. I broke down outside of the courtroom. I did not understand what was happening to me, and the caseworkers were doing their level best to help me. Let us just say it was not sinking in so as to help me feel better.

The judge came out of the courtroom, started patting me on my back, and explained to me that my parents terminated their rights to me. The Judge said, "Termination of parental rights means the end of a legally recognized parent-child relationship. If your parental rights to your child are terminated, you will no longer have the legal right to any contact with the child, in person or by telephone, mail, or computer." I stood up next to the Judge, looked at him, and said, "That's it"? The Judge replied, "Yes, it is." I could not even cry anymore. There was no hope for this day to get any better. I was truly lost. I started playing flashbacks in my head of the family I had. Even though my mother was not the best at dealing with me, they were still my family.

Sadly, my sisters did not even come to see me for the last time. Why I expected them to is beyond me. The more I thought about it, the worse I felt. At that moment, I was still crying. I told myself I was going to make it without parents and without family. However, I had to let my heart and mind heal first. Because of what had just happened, I was allowed to pick where we were going to eat. McDonald's was my favorite place to eat. The good thing was I was able to eat my food. My emotions were still running high. I wanted my family to understand I was not going to grow up without realizing what had happened in the courthouse. I was troubled at heart because no one had the decency to tell me anything about it.

I just kept running things through my mind repeatedly, until I was upset once more. I was no longer able even to enjoy my meal. I sat and watched everyone at the table, talking and laughing, as if I had not just lost my family. The fear in the life of losing family twice now made me wonder if I ever would know what a happy family life was like. I was a bit angry watching these folks laugh and have fun. However, I knew that it was not my fault, nor was it theirs either. Church had taught me that if I lived by God's Word that in the end, generally, things will turn out for the better. I would enjoy that happy family life one day.

CHAPTER 8 Growing Up Adopted

I have no idea who my biological father is. I do not personally know my biological mother, who abused alcohol and drugs and ended up getting pregnant with me while being locked up in a rehabilitation center. I was put in foster care and know nothing of that early life. I was adopted into a house of horrors where I was tortured and punished with beatings until I bled for the next nine years, for things that other children might get a stern talking or lose their cellphone for a week.

My adoptive father was the one who although being deathly ill my entire stay, tried to love and protect me from the matriarch of the house, who literally ruled with an iron fist. It does bother me at times that my biological parents were not able to care for me and, love my, that my mother had to be a drug addict. It is as though I was not worth the effort for them to make life changes for me. At other times, I feel sorry for her, as she may have had to deal with tragedies in her own young life, and may not have had the opportunities that I was given. I do wonder about what look she might have on her face and of how she would react to my being a success regardless of the odds against me, for which I give all of the credit to our Heavenly Father.

Even though I am an adult now, I still sometimes wrestle with the feelings that I am not as valued as those who were raised by their biological parents. Occasionally, someone will say something like, 'you should be grateful that you were adopted and have wonderful parents who were moved to adopt you.' Of course, I am getting ahead of myself because Adoptive Parent Part II is coming. However, in addressing this common comment, I am very grateful, but comments like these can make an adoptive child feel like there is something wrong with them and it took some kind of extraordinary effort for them to be loved.

My Adoptive Parent Part II is a loving, caring conservative Christian woman, who has given me the gift of God's Word. I think of the Psalmist's comforting thoughts, "For my father and my mother have forsaken me, but the Lord will take me in." (Psalm 27:10, ESV) There is little doubt that this is true in my case because both my biological parents did not love me enough even to attempt to be there. Moreover, my first adoptive mother utterly rejected and hated me from day one and showed me just how much through beatings and any mistreatment she could think of.

One thing that most adults who were adopted have in common is the desire to be loved. While this applies to all people, it is even truer of those who have been abandoned by their biological parents, only to be tossed around the foster care system. However, another trait that I have acquired is that I truly love people and I have this inner desire to help any who are hurting. Being a Christian, who has a ministry of talking about the Bible; it offers me the dignity and purpose I never knew the first eleven years of my life. When I feel a little depressed, I attempt to be helpful to others. By being a motivational speaker, who uses God's Word as his primary tool, I find that I can really connect with everyone because we all have a story to tell.

As we finished up at McDonald's, my case worker was talking with me and helping me understand what was about to happen and where I was going to be living from this point on. I was heading for an all-male placement home for children ages 5 to 18. I had no idea of how long I would have to stay there. So, here I sat in the van once more, with all of my black bags that contained my few belongings. I was now heading to a whole other way of life. Yes, some more difficulties before you the reader get to me my new adoptive mother and the life changes I will make.

CHAPTER 9 Jeff Jordan

Rebooting my life was happening yet again. We pulled up to the home that I was being placed in and it looked like a gold course, with the grass being nice and green, neatly cut. The houses were pretty neat looking to me as well. Then, I saw it that they had a basketball court. Well, maybe this was not going to be as bad as before. Regardless of what it would be like, I knew one thing for certain. I was going to make a real effort at turning my life around so that I would never lose a future family again.

The staff seemed to be very kind and welcomed me. They were eager to get me engaged in their program and events for my age group. I was very disappointed at how my parents threw all of my things in these big, black garbage bags, It was like a subtle message, as though they did not care and I meant nothing after being their son for nine years. I did still hold onto the hope of my parents and sisters wanting me back for a time, but that was dashed after I was assigned a new case worker. I will say that the therapy really lifted a lot of the pressure I was feeling.

I was here with a lot of others, many like me, who suffered through beatings, other still backgrounds where they suffered sexual assaults. Mistreatment from adoptive parents was the norm for those who were here so I cannot say it is the norm overall, but these placement centers are filled with such horror stories. These young ones like me were unable to deal with life, based on the pain and suffering that they had experienced. Mostly, they just wanted to crawl into a corner somewhere and never come out again.

The trauma built up from daily suffering over years of mistreatment leaves one with post-traumatic stress disorder. PTSD is a condition of persistent mental and emotional stress occurring because of injury or severe psychological shock, typically involving disturbance of sleep and constant vivid recall of the experience, with dulled responses to others and to the outside world. "Studies show that about 15% to 43% of girls and 14% to 43% of **boys** go through at least one trauma. Of those **children** and teens who **have** had a trauma, 3% to 15% of girls and 1% to 6% of **boys** develop **PTSD**. Rates of **PTSD** are higher for certain types of trauma survivors."[7]

PTSD is not just a soldier's disease. "According to a study conducted by The Harvard Crimson, et. al. One in four alumni of foster care experience PTSD and more than half

---

[7] PTSD in Children and Teens - PTSD: National Center for PTSD, http://www.ptsd.va.gov/public/family/ptsd-children-adolescents.asp?platform=hoot (accessed November 29, 2016).

experience at least one mental health issue such as depression, social phobia or panic syndrome. clearly expected to keep at-risk or abused children safe. ... trauma/s that caused PTSD."[8]

Simply put, I was in and out of foster homes for some time. While the experience was no way near my first adoptive parents, things still were very uncomfortable for a young child. Being shuffled from one home to another, being stair at in school, feeling like you are not worthy of life, having the biological kids of the house mistreat you, it all was nothing but more emotional trauma upon what I had gone through. I just wanted off this merry-go-round.

I was just in this constant mode of feeling that the trauma is happening again. I was experiencing bad dreams and nightmares. I also had a tendency to be very frightened by loud noises or by someone suddenly coming up to me from behind. This nervous feeling and sweatiness would not go away. There are times when my heart pounded, and I had trouble breathing. There are times when I would see, hear, feel, smell, or taste something that would cause the trauma to come rushing back into my life. There is the constant fear of being in that life again. I would have trouble controlling my

[8] Post Traumatic Stress Disorder; Not just a soldier's ..., http://www.fosterfocusmag.com/articles/post-traumatic-stress-disorder-not-just-s (accessed November 29, 2016).

emotions because reminders would lead to sudden anxiety, anger, or being upset. All of this made it difficult for me to concentrate on my schoolwork. Sleeping through the night was almost impossible too, which led to me being sleep deprived. I was agitated at times and in a constant state of being on the lookout for any danger or harm that might be coming my way. There were times when I would just emotionally shut down or felt an emotional numbness. While I wanted to be loved more than anything, it was hard to love or feel any strong emotional attachment to others after my first adoptive parents and numerous foster homes. At times, I just felt disconnected from the world that was around me, as if I was some kind of alien.

Either way, those of us who have suffered from PTSD, and those who want to help persons such as myself, they should remember that recovery requires patience. The apostle Paul encourages Christians to "console the discouraged,[9] support the weak, be patient toward all." (1 Thess. 5:14) I have come a long way since the helpless times of foster care

The Word of God is the ultimate tool in being able to cope with the stress of life in a foster family. God is "is full of compassion and

---

[9] Or the depressed; Lit *ones of little soul*

is merciful." (Jam. 5:11) If we keep our mind focused on the bigger scheme of things, like the will and purposes of the Father and the role that we can play in such, it will bring much comfort.

Think of the tender words of Jesus Christ from long ago and how they can refresh oppressed and stressed listeners, ""Come to me, all you who are laboring and loaded down, and I will give you rest. Take my yoke upon you and learn from me, for I am gentle and lowly in heart, and you will find rest for your souls. For my yoke is easy,[10] and my burden is light." (Matthew 11:28-30)

Good communication is one of the most valuable tools for managing their stress. The Bible teaches, "Without consultation, plans are frustrated, But with many counselors they succeed." (Prov. 15:22, NASB) Thus, many find that talking to the person that is causing them stress as a first recourse, or a friend if that fails, even talking to a mature one in the church; it will do much to reduce stress.

The apostle Paul tells us, "In nothing be anxious, but in everything by prayer and supplication with thanksgiving let your requests be made known to God. And the peace of God, which surpasses all understanding, will

---

[10] I.e. *easy to bear*

guard your hearts and your minds[11] in Christ Jesus." (Philippians 4:6-7)

4:6. Joy replaces anxiety in life, so Paul advises the Philippians not to be **anxious about anything**. The cure for anxiety? Prayer! Worry and anxiety come from focusing on your circumstances such as imprisonment or persecution which Paul and the Philippians faced. Anxiety or worry doesn't accomplish anything, but prayer does (Jas. 5:16). Jesus warned against worry which demonstrates a lack of trust in God (Matt. 6:25–34).

4:7. The peace of God comes from prayer involving both asking God for earthly needs and thanking God for his presence and provision. The expression appears only here in the New Testament. God's peace reflects the divine character, which lives in serenity, totally separate from all anxiety and worry. Such peace is like a squad of Roman soldiers standing guard and protecting you from worry and fret. Such peace is not a dream of the human mind. The human mind cannot even comprehend this kind of peace, wholeness, and quiet confidence. Such peace protects the two organs of worry—**heart** and **mind that** produce feelings and thoughts. Such protection is real, available in Christ Jesus.

---

[11] Or "your mental powers; your thoughts."

> Those who do not trust and commit their life to Christ have no hope for peace.[12]

There is no better support group than the Christian congregation. The author of the book of Hebrews writes, "And let us consider how to stir up one another to love and good works, not forsaking our own assembling together, as is the custom of some, but encouraging one another; and all the more as you see the day drawing near." (Hebrews 10:24-25)

Certain characteristics will enable one to live a less stressful life as well. Paul writes, "The fruit of the Spirit is love, joy, peace, patience, kindness, goodness, faithfulness, gentleness, self-control" (Gal. 5:22-23), as well as "Let all bitterness and wrath and anger and clamor and slander be put away from you, along with all malice. Be kind to one another, tender-hearted, forgiving each other, just as God in Christ also has forgiven you." (Ephesians 4:31-32)

> **5:22–23.** In contrast to the "acts of the flesh" presented above, those who are obedient to the Holy Spirit produce beautiful, nourishing spiritual fruit. Notice the fruit in this passage is called the fruit of the Spirit, not the fruit of self-

---

[12] Max Anders, *Galatians-Colossians*, vol. 8, Holman New Testament Commentary (Nashville, TN: Broadman & Holman Publishers, 1999), 261–262.

effort. This fruit the Holy Spirit produces in the life of a faithful Christian. In other passages of Scripture, we are commanded to fulfill the individual characteristics. The answer to this seeming paradox, I believe, is that only the Holy Spirit can produce the fruit; but he will not do so unless we are striving to the best of our ability for them in faithful obedience. These fruits of the Spirit are in harmony with and not opposed to the law. However, they are not produced by the law but rather by the Spirit working through the believer's faith.[13]

4:31–32. Christians are to "put away" five sins: bitterness, wrath, anger, clamor, and slander. In their place, they are to "put on" three virtues: kindness, tender-heartedness, and forgiveness. Because God acts this way toward us, we should act this way toward others. Then the church will be built up, the people will be holy, and Christ's body will be unified.[14]

---

[13] Max Anders, *Galatians-Colossians*, vol. 8, Holman New Testament Commentary (Nashville, TN: Broadman & Holman Publishers, 1999), 65.

[14] Max Anders, *Galatians-Colossians*, vol. 8, Holman New Testament Commentary (Nashville, TN: Broadman & Holman Publishers, 1999), 156.

CHAPTER 10 Where are the Keys?

While it is true that God will open doors for you, we need to understand better what role we play in this door opening process. Many times this is misunderstood. Let me set the tone for what I am about to say. Who will be receiving eternal life? Yes, this is a free gift that goes out to all who place their trust and have faith in Jesus Christ, and he alone decides. However, we do play a role, as the Bible says the righteous will get life, those walking with God will get life, those trusting in God will get life, so there are qualifiers. The biggest qualifier is what we will focus on here, Matthew 7:21-23. Notice what Jesus says in verse 21, "Not everyone who says to me, 'Lord, Lord,' will enter the kingdom of heaven." Well, who will? Jesus answers **only** "the one who **does** **the** **will** of my Father."

What should be our first question? Yes, what is the will of the Father? It is obeying the Word of God that he gave us. Then, why will some fail? What do you mean? Look at verse 22, "On that day many will say to me, 'Lord, Lord, did we not prophesy in your name, and cast out demons in your name, and do many mighty works in your name?'" The modern day reader can plug many things into what Jesus said, such as, "On that day many will say to me, 'Lord, Lord, did we not help the poor in your name, and start soup kitchens in your name, and do many different works in your name?'" You see if we plug in our will as to what we think God's will is; it does not work. What will Jesus say to the ones who believed that they were doing the will of the Father? In verse 23, "And then I will declare to them, 'I never knew you; depart from me, you who practice lawlessness.'" If we read our interpretation **into** the Bible, it is **our will** that we are doing. If we take the correct interpretation **out of** the Bible, it is the **will of the Father**. Let us look at some verses that seem like they are absolutes.

Earlier I quoted Philippians 4:6, which reads, "In **nothing be anxious**; but **in everything by prayer** and supplication with thanksgiving **let your requests be made known** to God." When Paul says, nothing should make us anxious, does he really mean that we should never be anxious about anything? A proper measure of anxiousness is actually good. It is only proper to be anxious about doing the will of God. The psalmist: "I am anxious because of my sin." (Ps 38:18, LEB) A proper measure of anxiousness concerning sin can lead us to confess them to the Father, turnaround from our former course, restore our relationship with the Father. Christians should be anxious, about the spiritual, physical, mental, emotional and material welfare of fellow believers. (1 Cor. 12:25-27) Jesus said, **"Do not be anxious** about your soul, what you will eat or what you will drink, nor about your body, what you will put on. Is not life more than food, and the body more than clothing?" (Matt. 6:25) Christians face enough problems each day without having undue anxiety about what will happen the next day. In fact, we may be worrying about what may never happen.

Returning to Philippians 4:6, Paul went on to say, **in everything by prayer ... let your requests be made known**. Does it really mean everything? No, only those things that are in harmony with the will of the Father. It is doubtful that a specific prayer request of a Cadillac Escalade is in accordance with the will of the Father. Therefore, our personal prayers may include almost anything, but the most important things should be about the Father's interests. When we are considering our concerns, "everything" can include our feelings, needs, fears, and anxieties.

Jesus also says, "Therefore do not be anxious, saying, 'What shall we eat?' or 'What shall we drink?' or 'What shall we wear?' For the nations eagerly seek all these things; for your heavenly Father knows that you need all these things. But be you seeking[15] the kingdom of God and his righteousness, and all these things will be added to you. Therefore, do not be anxious about tomorrow, for tomorrow will be anxious for itself. Sufficient for the day is its own wickedness." (Matt 6:31-34) Are these absolutes? No, there are plenty of Christians that have sought the kingdom, lived a righteous life, and had walked with God, yet they suffered through life, some died because of atrocious diseases, others were victims of a crime or natural disaster resulting in their death. Does this mean that Jesus lied, No, because there is only one absolute in the Bible, do the will of the Father and you will receive eternal life. The others are what will likely happen in great probability if you are doing the will of the Father, as opposed to what will happen if you are doing your will or the will of Satan's world. For example, 'if you are seeking the kingdom continuously, generally speaking, all these things will happen.' The Bible encourages frugalness (prudence in avoiding waste). If during a recession, a Christian only focuses on necessities and not wants, looks for sales, uses coupons, has a garden, shops at thrift stores, and the like; they are more likely to succeed as opposed to worldly person seeking their own

---

[15] Gr., zeteite; the verb form indicates continuous action.

desires. Does it mean that they will not suffer tremendous hardships? No.

The above is based on Bible studies, not just Bible reading. It means that we need to understand better the Word of God, to do the will of the Father. In the storyline, I am still young, and I did not make the right decisions that allowed doors to be opened. I had people coming into my life that could have helped me to make significant changes, but there are times when I rejected these ones. Therefore, in those moments, I was doing my will not the will of the Father. I was now in the seventh grade, still living in foster care. One day I was called to the principal's office and a man that had gone to church with my first adopted parents and me for years was sitting there. I was informed that my former adoptive father had died from kidney disease. This crushed my world. He was one of the first people to truly love me and defend me as best he could. While it was a momentary setback for me emotionally and with my getting into trouble, I still knew that I wanted to make life changes, to seek first the kingdom of God. There are some who struggle with learning from their mistakes, as did I for most of my youth. However, I was very observant as to why some people were succeeding in life and others were not.

The Perfect Fix Was In

My caseworker came through for me, working day and night to find me the perfect home. This came in 2007. I went on several home visits to what we felt was the perfect match. The mother was a loving woman, who cared deeply for young people. Everyone knew that I was now fifteen-years-old and did not want me to suffer from anymore jumping from one foster care place to another. They also did not want me to be a statistic. This family showed me the love that I had longed for so long, so I was moved into their home.

My new foster mother, Barbara, had three biological children of her own: two sons (Lionel and Baron) and one daughter (Malika). Only one of the sons still lived at home, along with another foster child. I and the other foster child shared rooms while her son lived across the hall. The difference here from my first foster family was night and day. My new foster mother wanted me to feel as though this were my home just as much as her and her family. My foster mother was a retired schoolteacher, who had a serious but great no-nonsense demeanor about herself. The other foster child did not stay long after I arrived. He was older and moved out on his own.

The great thing about my new foster mother was she made you feel welcome to the point where you could come to her about anything, at any time of the day, even if it were 3:00 AM in the morning. She was eager to guide you through the problems of life. Her children were older than I was and wanted to be a helpful part of my life, unlike times past, where biological children were abusive toward me. From here, when I say mother, I am referring to Barbara. Mother was also busy trying to help me as a person, teaching me how to cook full course meals, cleaning dishes, washing close by separating colors from whites and the like. Even her children were helping me along the way.

Six months after I moved in, I got a new foster brother, and his name was Michael. Both Michael and I were freshmen in high school. Lionel went to another school for smarter children. My mother was so proud of her son; she seemed to beam every time he came around. Whenever we hung out, we always had a good time. He was a brother that really wanted to make something out of himself and be a great foster brother towards me. I saw why my mother was so happy and thankful to have a son like that. Lionel was always willing to take me under his wing and try to teach me different things in life that I may not have known.

He was someone who I could truly call my brother. Our relationship as brothers grew stronger over time. Mom was starting to notice it in the home. It was also a lot of fun when Michael came around. However, he was not really into basketball, shopping, talking to girls and going out to the club like Lionel and myself. Of course, today, as a Christian, I realize many things I did back then would not be appropriate today.

That was okay, though, he was very different in the things he wanted to do, and he never wanted us to be involved. Lionel and I would support him, and we understood he had to get comfortable at first. Michael was in foster care for many years before me. We would share our stories with one another. The more we spoke, the more he was becoming comfortable sharing with me. I wanted to become that brother that Michael could come to just how I went to Lionel. We shared many differences, one of which was that he wanted short-term stay and I wanted long-term. There was nothing wrong with the way he would think just following his heart.

My brother Baron had a Chevy Impala (navy blue). I still did not know how to drive. I thought that Baron and I were close enough that he would let me drive. Michael and I used to talk about a way to get to drive while we were in our room. Michael really did not have any good ideas. They did not get any better even when I added the incentive of taking him wherever he would want to go. Eventually, we just decided that we would ask Lionel to drive his car instead of Baron. Moreover, we would take Lionel with us so he could see how well I drive. Well, it did not go as well as I had hoped. I got the nerve one day and asked, "Hey, Lionel, will you let me drive your car as long as you in the car with me?" Mother ended it within seconds, she said, "Not until you get your permit."

I still schemed with Michael about taking the car at night when Lionel was asleep. At first, I was not going to ask Michael if he thought that was a good idea because I figured he would tell mother. I just could not see any way of getting at his keys until it dawned on me that my mother left her keys out at night. She also had a spare key to Lionel's car with hers, which meant I could take the car at night.

Once I figured out when my brother would be asleep, I knew I would be in great shape to take the car and drive. The only way to figure that out was to go into my brother's room to get on his computer or talk with him and chill until he fell asleep. As you can see, I was still struggling with making the right decisions.

For a while, my attitude and emotions were still running bad. I had the attitude that I was going to do what I wanted to do. I even stopped doing my homework and paying attention in class, acting out as the class clown again. I had my fair share of trips to the assistant principal's office. The teacher even had me sitting right next to her desk for a time, as if I was in kindergarten again. This was just me trying to fit in, trying to follow others instead of what I knew to be right. I wanted to be like and dress like the so-called "cool" kids.

My freshman year was about me and trying to stand out in the crowd. The school actually contributed to my desire to be an important person. In the middle of the year, I was nominated for student of the month. After that, I was put on the honor roll for my who freshman year.

I didn't want others to be right about me. How can we let others judge us when they don't know us or our hopes for the future? That is when my actions started to show that I am somebody. The crazy thing was I was telling myself that and not worrying about the wrong things anymore. Time passed with my in this state of mind. I might have made some progress personally, but it was still coming too slow.

In 2009, my mother called me into her room to talk with her. Either I was in trouble or she wanted me to watch Family Feud with her. She said that she had spoken with the biological children and everyone wanted me to join their family. My face was priceless. I leaned over towards my mother's gave her a big hug and told her that, "I am so thankful." I would be honored to be a part of such a wonderful family. It was amazing how I came to this home not knowing what was going to happen, and now I was going to become a Jordan. My life was now going to make the transformation that I had always wanted. What took it to an entirely new level was I started listening to the older ones in my life. In my junior year, I again was on the honor roll and won another award. I still had some small scrapes with getting into trouble, but they were minimal and farther apart. With going to school and playing sports, such as basketball, football, and track and field, there were many times I would not get into trouble because I had something to do. In my senior year, I became class president of 2011.

CHAPTER 11 What Did I Do?

Coming to Western Kentucky University in the fall of 2011 as a college freshman would be a new beginning for me. With WKU being a well-known institution, I knew it was a good place for me to study and grow. It also would not be outside of Kentucky, and only an hour and thirty minutes from home. Coming to a conclusion on schools was easy. I did not want to stay in Louisville, so WKU was it. During the visit I had taken earlier that year to the campus, I saw how beautiful the campus was. My future was walking up and down the WKU Hill. I was excited to come to the University a week before my first year began to take part in Master Plan.

Master Plan is a program that gives a great advantage for all incoming freshman: to start visiting the campus and workshops, meet other freshman, and to get to campus a week before school begins. Coming from high school, where I was popular, to a campus with over twenty thousand students made me nervous. My dorm was in Barnes Hall. On move-in day, my mother, sister, brother, and a former social worker came with me to help settled into the next chapter of my life.

Once we arrive in Bowling Green, KY, we went to the nearby shopping center. It was a lot of fun. I had great support from everyone, and all of them helped me get everything I needed for my first year. My family left once I moved in the dorm. We all got emotional because I was not leaving with them; it was a good start for me. I could not believe this was happening to me making it to the next step in my life; and I was not supposed to be moving onto this level at all, based on statistics.

The tears were not sad tears; they were a moment of celebration. My former social worker and I stood and waved goodbye to my family as they headed back to Louisville. My social worker did not leave right away. Instead, she decided to treat me to one of her favorite restaurants, Red Lobster. As we were driving, I tried to figure out my way around. Melissa (social worker) was familiar with the Bowling Green area, and I was trying to catch up. Coming from a large city like Louisville, Bowling Green was very different, but Red Lobster was pretty much the same. In the middle of eating, I wondered why my family had to go back so early. It was only noon by the time we finish moving everything into my dorm. It was August, and the next time I would see them would be Fall Break, in October; unless they came to see me before then.

After eating, I was upset. Turned out Melissa stayed because she did not know either, and Melissa she always stood right by my side. By law, she was not even my social worker anymore. To me, Melissa is like a mother figure, friend, and mentor. When Melissa was taking me back to my dorm, I knew this would be it for a while, and emotions got a little heavy for both of us. After Melissa had left, I knew it was time to move on to meet new friends and peers.

During my first year, my roommate was cool, and I had a great time getting to know him; but he ended up transferring schools during the semester. While we were roommates, I would see his family come visit him and spend time with him unlike his, my family started to fade away, and I did not understand the reason. I would call them all the time, and I would get in touch either a day later or no answer. Whenever I saw, my roommate's family come visit him, I would call mine, but there was no reply from any of my family member. I started to get worried.

The first time I heard from my mother, she said that the whole family was coming to see me on the first college football game day. I was excited finally to get in touch with her, and that the family was coming as well. I was not sure why my brothers and sister were not returning phone calls or texts. I knew if I asked why they would not answer my phone calls or text messages, I would get some excuse.

Well, my family did not show up for the football game. They did not even give a reason why, nor did I get a phone call to inform me that they were not going to be able to make it. Here I was at a large school, alone, and they would not even come visit me, or ask how I was doing. Talking with Melissa, she did not understand what was going on either. My roommate would ask if my family was coming in for the small family events WKU would have, and I never knew. It was hard for me during my first semester of college. My sister and brothers ended up changing their numbers, without texting or calling to give me their new numbers.

Except for my college advisor, I lived without support. My first year of college was going to bring chaos if I did not get it together. I could not let not having my family in my everyday life affect my education. I knew being down, or trying to explain it to my teachers, or anyone else was not going to make anything better. Throughout my first semester, I tried to contact my family to inform them about the upcoming holidays and breaks that were coming up, to see if someone would come to Bowling Green, KY to pick me up. I got in touch with my mother a few times, and she said that either she or someone in the family would pick me up for any breaks. I felt good hearing that.

My school and studies got back on track, and my attitude toward everything started to improve. When October came, it was time for me to go home for my first break. However, once again no answer from my mother, and I still had not gotten my sister or brother's numbers. I would go four days at a time without a call or text from my family, without knowing how I am going to get home to see them. I had no way of getting back to Louisville.

To make a long story short, I ended up going on fall break with my new roommate and his family. They opened their arms, as they understood everything about my life. At that moment thinking about the desperate situation I was in, I got emotional. I could not believe my family bailed on me in my first semester as a freshman when I was only one hour and thirty minutes away. I could not believe this was happening to me. My roommate ended up becoming a close friend for many years. It was hard for me to accept that my family was treating me like this.

They know everything about my past, and that I was truly blessed to have them in my life.

Going home with my friend to Evansville, IN was a lot of fun. I had never been to that part of the country before. I heard Evansville city had many fun things to do, so I hoped this would keep my mind clear of my family situation. I was hoping that maybe they would call or something, but nothing.

I was feeling depressed, and I wanted to go home to my family in Louisville, but we were going in the opposite direction. I called my mother a few times to see what was going on and I still received no answer from her. There was nothing more I could do. I still had a good time on fall break with my friend. The support that my roommate and his family showed me was overwhelming.

CHAPTER 12 Figure It Out

Fall break for WKU was for three days, including the weekend. Spending time with his family, going out to the lake, and having the family show me different things was all fun; like, going to the waterfront, malls, camping, and more. However, everyone and I knew where I wanted to be. There were moments that Michael's parents would check on me throughout the day to make sure I was okay. At times, I just wanted to ask them if they would take me to my house in Louisville, but I felt that would be taking advantage of their kindness.

Throughout fall break, I was still making calls to my mother, and still getting nothing back. As much as I was thankful for my friend having me stay with them, I was ready to get back to campus. I had gotten used to doing everything for myself, so I believe that I did not need anyone's help with my life. I had everything under control. It seemed like every time I opened up to someone, they would just walk out my life. I was done getting hurt by everyone that came my way. I started to close doors to anyone who wanted to be part of my life. Nobody could understand me or the pain I was going through at that moment. I did not want to hear people tell me that everything was going to be okay. Going through a tough time as a young man and freshman in college, I really wanted to stop facing my excuses for life and make them the test of my future.

My roommate and his family wanted to take me into their family, but I was not going to let them. I told myself that this chapter in my life was all in God's plan and I hoped for what He wanted out of me. Jumping into another family's arms was not going to make me forget about what happened with my family. I started to ask what could be done now that I let my school and education go to waste. There was a short period during my first semester where I stopped doing work, which was another one of those rash decisions.

Getting back to finishing my first semester of college was important to me. Even though I did not have anyone to show my pretty good grades too, it felt good to know that I was not giving up. I was able to find someone who was able to understand where I came from my mentor, Former WKU Chief of Police Robert Deane. I met him in fall of 2011 while WKU treated me with the most respect and told me that the chief would help me through this tough time as a freshman, and even the rest of my time at WKU.

As I mentioned, he was now my mentor, but before meeting the chief, I was not so sure if I felt comfortable sharing my story. I was not big on telling my business and how I grew up and about, the way my life as a college student started. Even though I felt the need for someone other than my roommate and his family to know, I wanted to continue to keep everything to myself. It took me until the beginning of the spring semester of 2012 to build and seek out a relationship with the Chief. He was very open and honest with me, and he would hear my story and attempted to help me where he could. It made me feel not bad about things. He wanted to know if I had ever been interested in being a police officer, and my response was yes. He thought it would be cool to give me a tour around the police station.

Once the tour was over, I could tell there were more conversations on the way soon. As of now we still have great conversations, go to lunch, and he is aware of everything that had happened before and after we met. As life continued to move on from my first year, more problems and situations started to arise which were hard for me to handle. When I noticed I would be spending Thanksgiving and Christmas without family, I knew it would be hard for me. I was almost thinking of finding a girlfriend and letting her family take me in, maybe it would help me find peace.

A lot of the time, I spent sitting in my dorm room I spent wondering if this is, what God wanted out of me, to be alone, but have people like the Chief of Police in my life to help guide me through the next steps. I would always walk around campus and think about my future, knowing that my one stable family was now long gone. How would I go on? How could I finish my first year? Is my family even worried about me? I was thinking about it all. How could this be for me? Even though I made good grades and was focused on the rest of my first semester, thinking about this each day was hurting me.

A lot of us have something in our lives that we wish were not going on or could go another way. How do you handle it? I learned that putting friends that are more positive, mentors, and leaders in my life helped guide me in the right direction. My family was gone, but that did not mean no one else cared about me. It was always hard for me to understand that.

I would continue to give up and lose focus on school and the people that were starting to come in my life. Hope was not for me anymore. People would come into my life, and I would still have my wall up. I still did not care about what they wanted to see out of me, or the help they want to offer. Nobody was going tell me nothing that I wanted to listen too. These were all the thoughts that were popping in and out my head all the time. It was for the best within me that I could continue to have a better vision and outlook in life. Nothing was going to come easy: not a degree, not speaking, not a career job, and not money. I have learned you must put in the time and effort to learn from those who are willing to help.

During my time at WKU, I wondered where I would be in the next few years. Nothing was going right for me. That is when I started talking with my mentor about my vision for the next four years. I ended up finding and hanging out with friends that I went to high school with. Researchers say if you go off to college in the same state as your high school classmates, there is a seventeen percent chance they are at the same university as you. Sure enough, there were old football teammates at WKU. Even though they were a few years older than I was, from that forward, we all started hanging out together. These guys stayed around me all the time. We ended up becoming close. Once I told them about my family situation, they could not believe it was same mother and family they had met in my high school days.

They helped give me hope, knowing I was not alone anymore. However, I would want to find a way to make excuses for myself to believe that I was alone. Leaving people like my friends every day made me wonder if they would continue to hang with me the next day or even in the next month. They made it clear to me that they told their families about my situation and they did not care if I came to stay with them anytime I was off from college or in town. I had real friends that went out of their way to make things happen the right way for me, and it was only right that I return the favor.

I knew my friends were older than I was, but was not sure when they were graduating from college. Until one day, we all went to the restaurant off campus called Cheddars. As we were waiting to be seated, we were having a conversation about the weekend ahead of us. We sat down and several people we knew from campus and from Louisville that I have not seen in a couple years were sitting right across from us. One thing I noticed coming from a bigger city to WKU is that you would not run into everyone you knew in a big city. However, in Bowling Green, it's quite the opposite. The guy I ran into was my best friend growing up, and our families were close at one time before I left. I made sure I had gotten his number before he left Cheddars; I thought that was the reason why I ran into these folks.

My friends would warn me on occasion not to hang with the wrong crowd on campus. Of course, I knew right from wrong I had been dealing with that all my life. However, I knew now my act was coming together to be something better. As an incoming sophomore, I was still learning things about the campus, and I knew listening to these guys was important since they knew what they were talking about. During this time, classes were getting harder because my mind was going everywhere. I found some guys who lived in the same dorm as me, and we started hanging out together. They were part of a big party group on campus. Of course, I wanted to fit in. One thing I learned was that to be a part of something major on campus was a great way to meet other people. However, this need to fit in is not something anyone should strive for because bad associations can ruin any progress that has been made, as you will see below.

I told my friends from high school that I had met some friends from my dorm and of course they told me I should watch out who I hang with. Going to parties and finding girls was my goal then, and schoolwork was not my primary focus. I wanted to stay "cool" and "popular" so that everyone around campus would respect me and know that I am cool with the big party group on campus. Many of us get lost in our own little worlds and do not see the bigger picture. I knew being a part of a partying group was not where I needed to be. There was no personal growth for me hanging with these folks.

There was still one moment in my sophomore year where I was giving up and losing hope. I would pray each day for God to show me the way and I just was not getting an answer. It goes back to doing the will of the Father, which I spoke of earlier. There was a time when I needed money, and I knew I could have asked a friend for a few dollars. However, I wanted to do everything by myself, with no help. I went to Taco Bell one day after classes. I usually went with my roommate, but he was not in the mood for it that day. If I did go, it was always through the drive thru. This time I decided I was going to go, eat inside. As I walked in, I wonder why I was eating Taco Bell alone. I found myself sitting next to a big window.

After I say my grace, I looked up and saw that there were not many in the restaurant, only a few employees sitting around eating their lunch. The dining area started to leave and even the employees returning back to work. I was finishing eating when I saw something nearby on the other table ahead of me: a colorful flower looking wrist type of wallet sitting by itself. As someone, that was still learning things in life, one problem that I still had was "the desire of my eyes" wanted to have control and win every time. (1 John 2:15-17) I kept looking over at the employees, who were laughing and joking around with each other. I was not sure what I was getting ready to do.

I knew I needed money and I was quick to feel sorry for myself, trying to excuse my bad thinking and behavior. I kept wondering if someone was going to come get the wallet, but not a soul came back for it, and I was ready to go. Nevertheless, I was not going to let my mind tell me I was not going to get this wallet. Not once did I believe that I was going to be a good citizen and turn the wallet into the employees. I needed money, and I thought that if I got ahold of this wallet that I get out of there with no worries. I went to get another refill for my drink and sat back down just to make sure. Ten minutes had passed when I decided to go for it and grab the wallet.

That is what I did. Once I got into my car, I had no idea what I was about to get into when I opened it. My mind was not on anything else besides finding a way to get by with what I believed at that time in my life, not that bad of a thing. I thought about those who committed the most serious crimes, like murder, robbery, selling drugs, or doing things that would lead to jail. However, taking that wallet is all I would do. As I opened the wallet, I was looking for cash, and sure enough, there were a few dollars and a debit/credit card. I was not for sure what I was getting ready to do. I needed food and other things. I was scared to swipe a debit card anywhere, and the cash was not enough to get anything.

I thought if I were to swipe any of the cards in that wallet, I would just trash them once I finished using them. My nerves started to worry me, but I believed I was not going to be caught. I wanted to tell my friends what I was about to do, but in my mind, I was trying to get by in life. Taking money from someone or stealing clothes, drugs, or food was not the mindset I planned to have when I needed money or help. The things I wanted to have, I did not need. All, To be honest, all I wanted was things that I could show off to other people. In my head money was everything. I went from Taco Bell to a big market store to see what I could get from those debit cards. The whole time I thought that I had no clue what the card's pin was.

I thought this was going to make this work. Sure enough, as I was walking around in the store, I saw a friend that I had been going to parties with. I stopped him and told him what I did over at Taco Bell. This reaction was typical, he was down with me stealing someone's wallet, and for that, I didn't even feel alone anymore. Therefore, we went shopping. I told my friend that we should not get everything, but of course, I went for the highest ideas. I knew that if I got all of the stuff it was going to make me happy, just for the moment. I had nobody telling me that what I was doing was wrong and that it may catch up with me. I had friends in my life that said this, but of course, I was not picking up the phone to let them know that I was making a bad mistake. The things I believe were right, were right, and nothing was going to get in my way. I actually believed that. Sure enough, one of the debit cards was declined. I tried running it as credit, but it did not work.

I tried to take some stuff off the total price, but no. I was ready to leave everything right there and walk out. It did not even ring in my head that I had these other cards with me. I pulled out another card and swiped it. The word "APPROVE" popped up and I was ready to get out of there. I knew I made a mistake, but I could not let my rational thinking get in the way in front of my friend. As we were leaving, I threw the card in the trash can right by the exit door. I could not believe it worked and I just wanted to hurry and get to my car, load the stuff, and pull out. Then, I thought to myself, I do not have any money, gas, or any food. Once my friend got into his car, he notices that it was out of gas too. We decided we would take one last chance with the card and swipe it for gas.

I was still without food as we threw away the card at the gas station. At that time, it was not a problem. I kept thinking that we should not be doing this. I just kept putting myself in a deeper hole as this day went on. I wanted to take it all back and start back at the moment I was looking out the window at Taco Bell. I knew I was lost in the moment and I wanted God to step in my life, but I was letting myself be a fool. How was that going to happen? Doing so in front of my friend, I would be a punk for sure. I knew if I did the right thing, I could be a better leader for myself and to others, but I was not sure that I was ready for that moment since I was making excuses for myself.

After that day had ended, I decided I would play with the new items I had gotten from the store. While doing so, I had to tell one of the friends I went to high school with to see what they thought. Talking on the phone with my friend, he did not sound pleased at all. He wanted me to return it. He was not happy with me. He wanted to meet me first thing next morning to see how he could help. I did not understand why he wanted to help me in the first place. In my eyes, this was a way to be caught.

Once we hung up with each other, I started to feel guilty. I just wanted to go to sleep, and not think about it. We have all been there when we know we have done made a mistake and do not know to fix it. We make mistakes, we all sin, we all can do better in our own right, and we all have someone that we can call or talk to that can steer us back around, but it's up to us to know what to do with it. Lying in bed, I just knew I had messed up. I asked myself how I was going to fix it.

The next day came, and I met my friend on campus to talk over breakfast. As I walked into the student center, there came my others friends along with the friend I spoken with over the phone. We started to eat breakfast, and I was not sure if Drake told the fellas what was up or not. So, we started to talk, and they saw that I was very quiet while we ate. One friend asked, "What's going on Jeff?"

Of course, I was ashamed. I went on to share with them what had happened, and the friend I told over the phone was no happier hearing me say it face to face. I could not believe the situations I put myself in by using my past as a crutch. I just felt like was in some serious trouble with the law. There was not one excuse, which was going to make this better. Something I learned talking with my friends was that they were going to keep it real and honest with me.

They could see how unhappy I was after they spoke to me. My friends informed me that they were not going to look down on me because of the mistake I made. I knew it would be best to call my mother, to inform her of what happened, but she still hadn't been answering or calling back. It had been over a year since that I spoke to or saw my family. I was hungry for help and talking with my mentor and friends was helping. I just needed to take a deep breath and know that if I changed courses and my way of thinking, all was going to be okay. Being worried and stressed was not going to make anything better.

CHAPTER 13 The New Path

In 2014, I joined Living Hope Baptist Church. Every part of me loves my church. Going to that church to worship has a great outreach for me to build, meet, learn and grow of where God is asking of me as a believer and where he is calling me to serve. Many in life do not know what they want to do in their service to God, but it goes back to finding out what the will of the Father is and doing it. Even though I'm not connected to my biological family, I couldn't be happier to have a great church family and the few people I have very close in my corner. I know for me, better and more positive relationships start in the church.

I heard Les Brown say, "Let your purpose be within you." In other words, keep pushing towards where your purpose could be. I never seen this gift happening for someone like me only because I did not know my purpose and place God wanted me to go. My irrational thinking from my being raised in a traumatic life disallowed me to grow for some time. Yet, each year, I continued to grow in some way, which I credit to my church and to all of the people who played a role in my life.

Paul often spoke of the conflict within the fallen, sinful flesh, and used such expressions as "the inner man" (Rom. 7:20), "our inner man is being renewed" (2 Cor. 4:16), and "with power through His Spirit in the inner man." (Eph. 3:16) These expressions are true because Christians have been 'renewed in the spirit of their mind.' (Eph. 4:23) The thinking of a biblically minded Christian, with the mind of Christ, is a spiritual direction. These ones have "laid aside the old self with its evil practices, and have put on the new self who is being renewed to a true knowledge according." (Col. 3:9-10, NASB) They are no longer 'conformed to this world, but have been transformed by the renewing of your mind.' (Rom. 12:2) Paul says of Christians, "we do have the mind of Christ." By getting the mind of Christ, who reveals the Father and his will and purposes to Christians, they are spiritual men and women. (1 Corinthians 2:14-16) I had some more learning to go through but that past year has really brought me through this renewed mind.

In 2015, after a long day of classes, I called my friend Drake to see if he wanted to get a bite to eat. Drake met me at Taco Bell. Before we went into this Taco Bell, I told him that I wanted to give back to someone who is without now. He grabbed and hugged me, as he was proud that I wanted to do that. I knew in my heart that I made a mistake by taking something that was not mine. I also spoke with my mentor Chief Deane on being a part of a local church. I grew up in church, I now found myself out of church once I came to college, which I knew needed to be changed.

A few months went by; it was a few weeks before spring break and what I had done a few months back was no longer heavy on my mind. My friends did not say anything about it. I was back on the right track, not making any excuses for myself, just ready to enjoy spring break in Miami. I had my friends with me all day, every day leading up to the trip. I still had no contact from my family, though. I was taking my biggest trip as a college kid, over eight hundred away, and it seemed like they did not even care anymore.

The trip was my get away. I was so excited I had a countdown on my phone. We were leaving at midnight, and we were driving fifteen hours. The weather was going to be in the eighties on the beach. I could not wait. When the countdown was over, I knew the trip was going to be fun with the fellas. Many things needed to be done before we left, such as a haircut, get a rental car and get prepared for the drive later that night. The trip there was not bad at all; we had a ball and got to Miami unharmed. It was a fantastic trip with the guys. I would enjoy going back there some day. Each day is a beautiful thing. That is an excellent way to look at life.

On April 16, 2015, my life was starting to feel more open. I received support from others. I was honored to receive The Jefferson Award. I got it for outstanding achievement in community service and for giving back to the community. It was exciting. I will never forget such an honor. Leading up to this event, I had three interviews with the newspapers for the day of the event. I had done some research on the Jefferson Award and I knew it was for me. I started to share with some of my mentors about the award and all them told me, "Yes, this award is truly for you. You deserve something this for yourself." I really started praying for this honor. This is how I felt at the time. I realize now that was much of my haughty spirit because one does not pray to be honored, nor does a humble Christian even seek to be honored. Clearly, praying to be honored is not doing the will of the Father; it is seeking one's own glory.

Even so, back then, I was getting very excited about this and knowing that this award is an honor to have not just for me but also for the local community. The direction my future was taking me is a big reason why I am giving back to the local community. Helping youth in school and connection with them on a personal level is just a passion of mine, wanting to see the growth in our young people. We need more folks in our community to help our youth and bring them together.

Returning to the apostle Paul, who continues in his talk about the "physical man," referring to the fleshly man. This one is unable to understand the Spirit fully. Jesus has brought me into the light, where things were formerly hidden in the darkness of my irrational thinking; he has now disclosed the purpose of the will of the Father to me. I have entered yet another new path in my life.

CHAPTER 14 The Process

I am asked a lot how did you change for the better in your life Jeff?

There really is not a direct answer. First, I am a true believer in God. God is doing all the work for my life, and all glory goes to Him. The way I started making a difference in life was by changing my everyday routine. I started getting on my knees and praying for a change in my daily life. I began believing in the change for my life. Following the great leadership inside the church helped me become more open.

Coming to church was not easy for me just coming from experience in growing up in the church, and how my life changed and I stopped going. There were many times when Jeff Jordan, who had no spiritual side to his life, who followed the desires of the human self to the rejection of spiritual things. In the end, our love for God, our obeying his commandments and our faith in the ransom sacrifice will result in our complete relief from the adversities that this imperfect life has thrown at us and we will be led to a lasting joy. (1 John 5:3)

In the meantime, we can draw comfort in knowing that the Creator is well aware of all the things that afflict us. King David wrote, "I will rejoice and be glad in your steadfast love because you have seen my affliction; you have known the distress of my soul." (Ps. 31:7) The Father is moved by his love us and our heartfelt desire to do His will, se he will rescue us through the adversities and calamities of life. (Ps. 34:19) However, it might not be in the way that we think. Jesus tells those of us who believe a fully trust Him: "If you **continue in my word** you are truly my disciples, and you will **know the truth**, and the **truth** will **set you free**." (John 8:31-32, LEB) The Father rescues us through His Word, the Bible. If we obey, we will succeed in life and be on the path to life; however, if we are sluggish abut obeying and are imposing our will on God's Word, Jesus will say, "'I never knew you; depart from me, you workers of lawlessness.'"

I walked through these doors coming from the school bus. Each bus had a color.

I ran away from home several times to this playground. This playground was in our local subdivision.

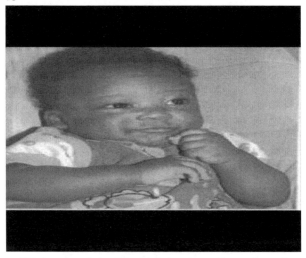

This is me as a baby. The only baby picture I have of myself.

This is the church attend and work at. What a great parking lot, right?

What does it mean to be a leader?

People, who can teach, guide, protect, listen, learn and grow. There are so many ways to lead like a shepherd for instance. When I am speaking to a group of people, or even just one person, I believe the power that the Word of God gives me is only to get that group or person to know what is ahead of them in a positive manner. Hebrews 4:12 tells us that "the word of God is living and active, sharper than any two-edged sword, piercing to the division of soul and of spirit, of joints and of marrow, and discerning the thoughts and intentions of the heart."

Our Leader, Jesus Christ, has given the Christian congregations "gifts in men": "some as

101

evangelizers, some as shepherds and teachers."
(Eph. 4:8, 11-12) The way we view them and
our actions toward them says a lot as to
whether we accept Christ's leadership. We are
to "be thankful" for the qualified leaders that
Christ has given us. (Col. 3:15) They are also
worthy our respect. The apostle Paul wrote,
"The elders who lead well must be considered
worthy of double honor, especially those who
labor by speaking and teaching." (1 Timothy
5:17, LEB) The author of Hebrews wrote of
leadership, "Remember your leaders, those
who spoke to you the word of God. Consider
the outcome of their way of life, and imitate
their faith." (Heb. 13:7, ESV) He went on to
say, "Obey your leaders and submit to them,
for they are keeping watch over your souls, as
those who will have to give an account. Let
them do this with joy and not with groaning,
for that would be of no advantage to you."
(Hebrews 13:17, ESV)

The Greatest Leader to Ever Live

The finest compliment that one can ever
receive is when another person imitates them.
Therefore, we ought to emulate the greatest
Leaders, who have ever lived, Jesus Christ!
How can we imitate Jesus as a leader? How
will our lives be impacted by accepting his
leadership? One way is by looking at the life of
the apostle Paul, who exemplified Jesus in his

life as an imperfect human. I would recommend, *Called to Lead: 26 Leadership Lessons from the Life of the Apostle Paul* (Sep 5, 2010) by John F. MacArthur

Consider How You Listen

How well do we listen to others? Do we really listen at all? Or, are we the one who interrupts abruptly with pat answers to problems that we have only surface knowledge of, just because we like to impress. Proverbs 18:13 says, "If one gives an answer before he hears, it is his folly and shame." When a conversation is taking place, there is a time to speak, and there is a time to be quiet, so as to listen better.

Thinking Ability

Knowledge is related to our thinking ability. Thinking ability can come in a depraved sense (sinful ideas, devious, and conniving schemes) or a positive sense (perceptiveness, insight, good judgment, and godly wisdom). Therefore, our imperfect human minds can be can be focused on a commendable, upright person or thing, or the opposite. If we are grounded in the Word of God, not just surface knowledge, paying attention to the things read and heard, we can protect our thinking ability. A person with the mind of Christ will have great thinking ability, and will not be ensnared by the desires of the eyes, heart, and mind. (1 Corinthians 2:16; 1 John 2:15-17)

Finding the Path

Proverbs 10:17 says to us, "Whoever heeds instruction is on the path to life, but he who rejects reproof leads others astray." One Bible scholar says of this verse "is a warning to follow the example of the wise rather than the wicked."[16] Another Bible scholar offers, "Our response to **discipline** affects others who see our example. If a person maintains a teachable spirit and chooses to pay attention to discipline, he will show others how to stay on the path that leads to **life**. But if he refuses to learn, he will lead **others astray**, with disastrous results."[17]

Trust In Him

John 3:16 (UASV) says, "For God so loved the world that he gave his only-begotten Son, in order that everyone **trusting in** him will not be destroyed but have eternal life."

On this verse Kenneth O. Gangel writes, "Before moving on with his narrative of Jesus' ministry and message, John wanted to state one more time the essence of the gospel—believing

---

[16] Duane A. Garrett, *Proverbs, Ecclesiastes, Song of Songs*, vol. 14, The New American Commentary (Nashville: Broadman & Holman Publishers, 1993), 119.

[17] Anders, Max. Holman Old Testament Commentary - Proverbs (p. 128). B&H Publishing. Kindle Edition.

people receive eternal life; rejecting people receive **God's wrath.** What is the wrath of God? By his very nature which is perfect, God opposes the disobedience and rebellion which come from unbelief. The word *orge*, from which we get our English word *orgy*, describes the anger of disapproval. It can arise gradually and is usually guided by reason and understanding. Hundreds of passages in the Bible refer to God's wrath. Morris quotes Hodgson: "The wrath of God and divine punishment are essential elements in a doctrine which is to face the facts of evil and retain a fundamental optimism. The belief that God has sworn in His wrath that men who do certain things shall not enter into His rest enables the Church to open its worship each day with the words, 'Come let us sing unto the Lord. Let us heartily rejoice in the strength of our salvation' " (Morris, p. 250). Any approach to God apart from Jesus Christ is futile. Religions, cults, and civic groups miss the message of the Bible when they talk frequently about God but do not want to disturb the pluralistic harmony of their members by emphasizing Jesus Christ. God allows no approach to himself apart from his Son. Whoever rejects the Son has forfeited eternal life and receives instead the wrath of

God. This is what the Bible means when it says life is in the Son."[18]

Jesus warned us, "Enter through the narrow gate; for the gate is wide and the way is broad that leads to destruction, and there are many who enter through it. For the gate is small and the way is narrow that leads to life, and there are few who find it." On this verse, Stuart K. Weber writes, "The **narrow gate** is the way of personal faith in Christ. This is precisely what the Pharisees missed so badly (Matt. 5:20). The Pharisees used the **wide ... gate**, which is the normal human tendency toward dependence on self-righteousness. The number of people who would, historically, find the narrow way has by now mounted into the millions, if not billions. But Jesus' **few** is a relative term. The true servant of the kingdom will always be in the minority."[19] What path will you choose?

Romans 8:28 Updated American Standard Version

28 And we know that all things work together for good for those who love God, for those who are called according to his purpose.

---

[18] Kenneth O. Gangel, *John*, vol. 4, Holman New Testament Commentary (Nashville, TN: Broadman & Holman Publishers, 2000), 60–61.

[19] Stuart K. Weber, *Matthew*, vol. 1, Holman New Testament Commentary (Nashville, TN: Broadman & Holman Publishers, 2000), 100.

8:28. The purposes of God are the most important reality in the spiritual life. The purpose (*prothesin*) of God's will is what controls everything (Eph. 1:11) in light of eternity (Eph. 3:11). God **called** us to a holy life on the basis of his purpose and grace, and it is that purpose to which we have been **called** that verse 28 invites our submission (God's calling here is not the calling of the many in Matt. 22:14, but the effectual calling to salvation of Rom. 11:29; 1 Cor 1:9; Eph. 4:4; 1 Thess. 2:12; 2 Tim. 1:9; and 1 Pet. 2:9).

Our new life in the Spirit is based on God's good purposes for our lives, and that includes suffering. The suffering (v. 17) and groaning (v. 23) that Paul has been discussing is what is in view in verse 28. When we find ourselves in trying circumstances in life, we can **know that in all things God works for the good of those who love him, who have been called according to his purpose**. Read literally, it is easy to see why some consider this the greatest verse in Scripture. It tells us that nothing happens outside of God's plan for our good.

An important grammatical question clarifies the role of God in accomplishing his purposes. "All things" can be taken either as the subject (as in KJV; "all things work together"), or as the object (NIV [adverbial], "in all things God works"; NASB [direct object], "God causes all things to work"). As the subject, "all things" are in control, and while they end happily, they do so seemingly in and of themselves. When God is the subject, he causes (*sunergei*, from *sunergeo*, to work with) all things to work together for good. In other words, there is no doubting the outcome's ultimate good. Lest we translate according to our theological preferences, it must be noted that (a) there is not a compelling grammatical reason to translate one way or the other (see the commentaries for minor possible reasons), and (b) the meaning is not radically altered with either translation.

It should probably be agreed with Moo that the plainest rendering of the text is that of the KJV ("all things work together for good"), but that "it does not finally matter all that much" between the choices mentioned above (Moo, p. 528). The reason is that **God** and **his purpose** are the controlling elements of the verse. Paul is clearly subordinating **all things** to the **purpose** of God, regardless of how the verse is written.[20]

Share your message!

[20] Kenneth Boa and William Kruidenier, *Romans*, vol. 6, Holman New Testament Commentary (Nashville, TN: Broadman & Holman Publishers, 2000), 259–260.

CHAPTER 15 How Can You Deal With the Challenges of Being Adopted?

The suggestions below are to be applied whether a loving family adopts you or the family ends up being an unloving family. Many times, our actions can change how others deal with us. And, of course, there are those times where we are the only one doing right in a relationship, and we must simply keep doing so because that is our obligation as a Christian.

Honor Your Father and Mother

Deuteronomy 5:16 tells us that we are to "Honor your father and your mother." We "honor" our adoptive father and our mother by being of strong moral character or strength, and adhering to biblical principles. We also show them great respect and admiration, even if they may not be worthy of it. We need to be kind to our adoptive parents, respecting them as a person, listening to what they have to say, and carrying out any reasonable requests that they make to you.

However, what if an adoptive parent asks you to do something that is unreasonable? This will likely happen because even biological parents will make unreasonable demands at times because we all are imperfect humans after all. The imperfection of others can make it difficult to be obedient all of the time. The problem is adoptive children will focus on the fact that they are adopted believing that this is why their parents are so unreasonable, and does that mean that you do not have to obey. You think to yourself, "I am not doing that, you never ask your biological children to do that." Should that really be how you deal with it?

It might help if you consider Jesus, who was a perfect child. (Heb. 4:15; 1 Pet. 2:22) However, Jesus adoptive father, Joseph, who was the husband of Mary, and later, the natural father of at least four sons, James, Joseph, Simon, and Judas, besides daughters. (Matt. 1:16; 13:55, 56; Lu 4:22; John 1:45; 6:42) You see Joseph was not perfect like Jesus. And Jesus mother, Mary was imperfect as well. Jesus being a perfect human being like Adam would have been far more intelligent as a child than any adult that he encountered. In fact at twelve years old, on one trip to Jerusalem for the Passover, he was accidently left behind. When Mary and Joseph came looking for him, they found him after three days in the temple **questioning** the Jewish religious leaders, men who had the equivalent of our Ph.D. today. We learn two things from this account. Jesus was not asking questions like a twelve-year-old boy, he was questioning these men in an interrogative way. The Greek word is an intensified word, a legal term like a prosecuting attorney interrogating someone on the stand in a trial. (Luke 2:46-47)

However, we also learn something about how Mary corrected Jesus in a stern way, saying, "Son, why have you treated us so? Behold, your father and I have been searching for you in great distress." (Lu 2:48) Being perfect, Jesus would have known every instance when his parents were wrong. Did Jesus choose to rebel against his adoptive father or his imperfect mother's guidance? No. The Bible tells us that as Jesus was "obedient" or "in subjection to" his parents. (Luke 2:51)

Now, there are going to be many times when you and your adoptive parents are going to see things differently. You may feel that they are wrong. First, this happens all of the time in biological families as well. Children see things different from adults and in today's world, they believe they are in the right, and their parents are in the wrong. Thus, this has nothing to do with your being adopted. Second, you must recognize that you are imperfect as well. Thus, it is highly likely that you are going to be in the wrong more than an adult. So, do not allow your being adopted to cloud your judgment. At any rate, it is best to follow in Jesus footsteps and remain obedient and subjection to your adopted parents. (1 Pet. 2:21) This mindset will help you feel better when you are being asked to do something that seems unreasonable. Also, there is an even more important reason to be obedient to your adoptive parents.

The Bible says, "Children, be obedient to your parents in all things, for this is well-pleasing in the Lord." (Col. 3:20) Yes, you're being obedient makes the Father happy. (Prov. 27:11) In addition, the Father wants you to be obedient and in subjection to your adoptive parents because wants you to be happy too. Young ones are encouraged to obey when He adds, "that it may be well with you, and that you may live long on the earth." (Ephesians 6:3, NASB)

Growing Closer to Our Adoptive Parents

While honor and obedience are important, it will take more if you are to cultivate a close relationship with your adoptive parents. Like me, you certainly want to be a part of a warm and loving family. It is your adoptive parents, who are responsible for making this happen but you play a role in it too.

You need to seek out ways to draw closer. Show interest in them right from the start. As you see, family pictures ask them about them.

At meal times, ask them about themselves. If you are struggling with childhood issues, go to your adoptive parents with it when you see that they are relaxed. (Prov. 20:5) In addition, do not wait for them to give you things to do. Take the initiative by volunteering to help with housework and chores.

Will your finding out who your biological parents are, ruin your relationship with your adoptive parents? Generally, this is not the case. Most adopted children tend to see their adoptive parents as their real parents because inside they realize the love and sacrifice that these ones have made. In the United States, it used to be that adoptive agencies were slow to give out biological parent's information. However, today they see the value in doing so. Generally, some states will wait until they have had a request from both parties first. In other words, the biological parent needs to contact the adoptive agency, and the child needs to communicate with them as well before either party gets the other's information. Some adoptive children desire to meet their biological parents, while some do not. Neither is wrong. If you are one who does, seek the help of your adoptive parents and maybe the pastor of your congregation. Proverbs 14:15 says, "The sensible one considers his steps." Just make sure that you let your adoptive parents know that this is a case of curiosity and that your love for them will never be lessened.

Growing Closer to Our Heavenly Father

Like myself, many youths who have grown up in foster care, or who have been adopted, struggle with abandonment issues. These ones have high anxiety that they will lose their adoptive family the same way they lost their biological family and were shuffled from one foster family to another. The apostle John wrote, "There is no fear in love, but perfect love casts out fear." You do not need to let gloomy fears of losing your loved ones control you. Rather, taking the time to draw close to all in your adoptive family because is the perfect bond. Even so, build up your love for your heavenly Father, as he will never abandon you, even when you stumble, as we all do, many times.

Again, we return to Philippians 4:6-7, "In nothing be anxious; but in everything by prayer and supplication with thanksgiving let your requests be made known to God. And the peace of God, which surpasses all understanding, will guard your hearts and your minds in Christ Jesus."

4:6 ... "Do not be anxious about anything." Jesus spoke about anxiety in the Sermon on the Mount (Matt 6:25–34), where he stated the most common causes of anxiety. They are: physical attributes (v. 27); clothing (v. 28); food and drink (v. 31); and the future (v. 34). Even in contemporary life with its complexities, the same simple concerns cause anxiety. Prayer cures anxiety. Here three words describe prayer. Each contributes to a proper understanding of the comprehensive nature of the prayer life. The point, however, is that prayer relieves the problem of anxiety. The center of the verse is the significant part: Prayer is to be offered "with thanksgiving." The attitude of gratitude accompanies all true approaches to the Father.

4:7 The answer to anxiety is the peace of God. Paul made three statements about this peace. First, it is divine peace. He did not envision a situation where circumstances changed or external needs were met. This peace was a characteristic of God which invaded the Christian. Second, it "transcends all understanding." "Transcends" translates the word *hyperechousa* ("excellent"), which is found in 2:3; 3:8, and here in a compound form. Paul contrasted knowledge and peace at one point: Peace excels over knowledge. No doubt he had in mind situations where knowledge is insufficient. Sometimes it cannot explain, and sometimes explanations do not help. Peace, however, is always appropriate and meets the need of the heart. Finally, this peace will "guard your hearts and your minds in Christ Jesus." "Guard" is a military term, implying that peace stands on duty to keep out anything that brings care and anxiety. For these reasons, prayerful people are peaceful people.[21]

My reading and studying the Bible has greatly helped me in drawing closer to God and living a happy life, spiritual, and fruitful life. Have a close relationship with the Father is very important because He knows how we feel. Again, Psalm 27:10 says, "For my father and my mother have forsaken me, but the Lord will take me in." S. Edward Tesh and Walter D. Zorn write, "What trust! Greater either than the love of mother or father is the love of God. How beautifully Isaiah expresses this truth: 'Can a mother forget the baby at her breast and have no compassion on the child she has borne?

---

[21] Richard R. Melick, *Philippians, Colossians, Philemon*, vol. 32, The New American Commentary (Nashville: Broadman & Holman Publishers, 1991), 149–150.

Though she may forget, I will not forget you'
(says the Lord) (Isa 49:15)."[22]

Adjusting Incorrect Assumptions

The thinking ability that we spoke of earlier
can aid us in examining any false assumptions
that may contribute to our anger. For example,
you might feel as though your biological
parents gave you away because they felt there
was something wrong with you. We must
realize that this is not always the case and it is
more often than not, the biological parent felt
that they were doing the loving thing. Some
will never know what the motivation was, but
we should never assume it was a negative
reason. In many cases, the biological parent(s)
feel that they are offering their child a better life
because they are too young, or they are
struggling with an addiction.

Job suffered far more than any Bible person
that we know of, and he said, "till I die I will
not put away my integrity from me." (Job
27:5) We need to consider wise King Solomon's
words, "Be wise, my son, and make my heart
glad, that I may answer him who reproaches
me." (Prov. 27:11) "Proverbs mentions
repeatedly that a wise son brings **joy** to a
father's **heart** (10:1; 15:20; 23:15,24; 29:3).

---

[22] S. Edward Tesh and Walter D. Zorn, *Psalms*, The College Press
NIV Commentary (Joplin, MO: College Press, 1999), 234.

Godly children are your best credentials, and they will give you an **answer** for the critic who holds you in **contempt**."[23] "In other words, his son will either publicly disgrace the father or enable him to stand proudly before even his enemies."[24] "When children develop responsible character, they **bring joy** to both father and mother (see 17:6). The Lord designed family members to treat each other with mutual respect."[25] This applies to our relationship with our heavenly Father as well. Satan has been taunting God since the Garden of Eden, besmirching and bringing reproach on His great name. We can wisely obey the Father and bring joy to the Father so that he has a reply to the one reproaching Him.

The Importance of Being Loved

If we are part of the Christian congregation, we too can enjoy the fact that we have many spiritual mothers, fathers, sisters, and brothers who love us. Jesus said, "Truly, I say to you, there is no one who has left house or brothers or sisters or mother or father or

---

[23] Anders, Max. Holman Old Testament Commentary - Proverbs (p. 339). B&H Publishing. Kindle Edition.

[24] Duane A. Garrett, *Proverbs, Ecclesiastes, Song of Songs*, vol. 14, The New American Commentary (Nashville: Broadman & Holman Publishers, 1993), 219.

[25] Dave Bland, *Proverbs, Ecclesiastes & Song of Songs*, The College Press NIV Commentary (Joplin, MO: College Press Pub. Co., 2002), 246.

children or lands, for my sake and for the gospel, who will not receive a hundred fold now in this time, houses and brothers and sisters and mothers and children and lands, with persecutions, and in the age to come eternal life." (Mark 10:29-30) The pastors within the congregation can be like the righteous kings that ruled over Judah, "Each will be like a hiding place from the wind, a shelter from the storm, like streams of water in a dry place, like the shade of a great rock in a weary land." (Isa. 32:2) Never be slow to seek out the mature Christians within the church and share your problems with them. Share with them what is on your mind and heart.

Success Is Within Your Reach

Resist false and negative thinking. Proverbs 24:10 tells us, "If you faint on the day of adversity, little is your strength." Duane A. Garrett writes, "This text calls the reader to summon courage to face whatever challenges lie ahead. Difficult times can manifest one's lack of mettle, but this proverb is meant to encourage the reader *not* to falter in the face of adversity."[26] Max Anders writes, "Trouble reveals either our courage or our weakness.

---

[26] Duane A. Garrett, *Proverbs, Ecclesiastes, Song of Songs*, vol. 14, The New American Commentary (Nashville: Broadman & Holman Publishers, 1993), 199.

Problems are inevitable, and our responsibility in life is to meet each challenge with God's help. He has designed us to rise to the occasion and has promised to provide his strength. So when we **falter in times of trouble**, we simply demonstrate how inadequate we are. Our **strength** is **small**, so we need to lean on the Lord."[27]

The Way of Success

Psalm 1:1-3 Updated American Standard Version (UASV)

1 Happy[28] is the man
who walks not in the counsel of the wicked,
nor stands in the way of sinners,
    nor sits in the seat of scoffers;
2 but his delight is in the law of Jehovah,
    and on his law he meditates day and night.

3 He is like a tree
planted by streams of water

---

[27] Anders, Max. Holman Old Testament Commentary - Proverbs (p. 337). B&H Publishing. Kindle Edition.

[28] **Happy, blessed is**: (Heb. *asre*; Gr. *makarios*) *Asre* occurs 11 times in the Hebrew Old Testament and *makarios* 50 times in the Greek New Testament. Happiness and being highly favored by God characterize this joy. It is speaking of a person who is content, full of joy. This is not to be confused with the Hebrew word *barak* which means, "to bless," as in a divine blessing. The Hebrew barak and the Greek *eulogeo* is the act of being blessed, while the Hebrew *asre* and Greek *makarios* is the state or condition of the person who is being blessed, who is a highly favored one. – 1 Ki 10:8; Ps 1:1; 119:1-2; Pro. 14:21; 16:20; Matt. 5:3-11; 11:6; 13:16; Lu 1:45; John 13:17; 20:29; Ac 20:35; Rom. 4:7-8 to mention just a few.

that yields its fruit in its season,
    and its leaf does not wither.
In all that he does, he prospers.

1:1 The commendation is expressed in the opening words, **blessed is the man**. The term "blessed" does not imply that God has bestowed some particular favor; a different Hebrew term is used to indicate that. Rather, it means that the person has so conducted himself that a condition of blessedness has resulted. "Oh, the happiness *that man* experiences," the psalmist is saying. And it is a happiness that is very definitely related to conduct. The good life is attractive and brings real, not superficial, happiness.

The source of this happiness is twofold. First, it lies in the avoidance of all of the ways of the wicked. There are some things that a righteous man, a wise man, will not do. (He) **does not walk in the counsel of the wicked**, refusing to adopt their hedonistic philosophy or to be taken in by their devious casuistry.

The wicked are the godless. Isaiah says that they "are like the tossing sea, which cannot rest, whose waves cast up mire and mud," adding, " 'there is no peace,' says my God, 'for the wicked' " (Isa 57:20–21). **Or stand in the way of sinners.** Note the progression—"walks, stands, sits." That is the nature of involvement in sin. One begins by tuning in on evil counsel. He next ventures an occasional indulgence, in the presence of bad company, even if it means a violation of his conscience. Then, before he realizes it, his life is cast in the new mold; and the change has been so complete that he has become one of that circle who take delight in sneering at goodness and ridiculing religion. The righteous man habitually shunned all of this. The verbs, in the Hebrew, are *perfect* (completed action), indicating with the negatives what, all the while, he has never done, i.e., "who has never walked."

1:2 The state of blessedness or happiness in life finds its source more in what a person does than in what he refrains from doing. The wise man refuses to walk in the way of evil, not because he is bound by an oversensitive conscience but because he has chosen to walk a better way. When it is a matter of choice between the counsel of the wicked and the way of the Lord, for him it is no contest. He chooses the latter. To him **the law of the Lord** is not a burden to be borne, nor even an obligation to be met, but a **delight** to be enjoyed. It is a gift from the Creator of life providing instruction on how best to live in such a way as to find fullness of life and, consequently, happiness. In a word, happiness is not found by searching for it, not an achievement of the will; happiness is doing what is right. And God has revealed what right is. Any of us who ignores God's direction does so at great peril, for the law of the Lord alone gives meaning and direction to human existence. To abandon the Scriptures is to be left adrift on the sea of life without chart or compass.

On his law he meditates. The purpose of such concern for God's law is indicated in Josh 1:8—"that you may be careful to do everything written in it." The delight lies in doing the will of God, not just in knowing it. Thus Jesus would say: "Blessed rather are [Oh, the happiness to them!] those who hear the word of God and obey it" (Luke 11:28).

1:3 To indicate what it is like to walk in the way of God, the psalmist uses the figure of a luxurious tree **planted by streams of water**. The tree, thus situated, is enabled to do what is natural to it; **which yields its fruit in season**. Just so, vitality and fruitfulness are characteristics of the life of righteousness, not as a reward or enticement, but as a natural consequence of such a life. In bearing fruit, the tree is fulfilling the purpose for which it was created. The man of wisdom is doing the same, finding his purpose in life and life's fulfillment in doing the will of God.

Whatever he does prospers. This

statement appears to be a categorical assertion to the effect that the righteous man will never experience any reverses. However, human experience says the contrary (consider Job, for example), and elsewhere the Psalms deal with the suffering of the righteous. Dahood proposes an alternate translation: "Whatever it (the tree) produces is good." On the basis of the Hebrew text, this is possible. Charles A. Briggs and others translate: "So all that he doeth, he carries through successfully"[7]—or to a successful outcome—meaning that whatever he does will result in good. A righteous man, like a good tree, will bear good fruit. God's law of the harvest is immutable.[29]

At times, the weight of having gone through foster care and being adopted may seem difficult. It may even seem difficult to serve God at times. However, it will never be too difficult to handle. (Deut. 30:11) The Bible promises that if you remain faithful to God's Word, 'everything that you do will succeed' in the end, as long as you are doing the will of the Father. The apostle John tells us "The world 9wicked humankind] is passing away, and its lusts; but **the one who does <u>the will</u>** of God remains forever." Remember, you are not alone

---

[29] S. Edward Tesh and Walter D. Zorn, *Psalms*, The College Press NIV Commentary (Joplin, MO: College Press, 1999), 87–89.

in this. You have the support of God, your adoptive family, and the congregation. (Matt. 28:20; Heb. 13:5; 1 Peter 2:17) The Father is well aware of the difficulties that you face daily. (Ps. 55:22) With these ones backing you, along with your resolve and effort, you can enjoy a successful life now and for an eternally!

Lastly, I would Like to Thank

- Jewel Jones
- Pastor Tyler Wittmer
- Dan Edmonson
- Roy Hutchins
- Pastor David Head
- Reyn Judd
- Sherry Novelli
- Dr. Gary Ransdell
- Bayne Million

96612449R00074

Made in the USA
Columbia, SC
30 May 2018